# Flashpoints of Revival
## History's Mighty Revivals

# Flashpoints of Revival

## History's Mighty Revivals

*Geoff Waugh*

### *Revival Press*

An Imprint of

**Destiny Image**® **Publishers, Inc.**
**P.O. Box 310**
**Shippensburg, PA 17257-0310**

ISBN 0-7684-1002-9

For Worldwide Distribution
Printed in the U.S.A.

This book and all other Destiny Image, Revival Press,
and Treasure House books are available
at Christian bookstores and distributors worldwide.

For a U.S. bookstore nearest you, call **1-800-722-6774**.
For more information on foreign distributors, call **717-532-3040**.
Or reach us on the Internet: **http://www.reapernet.com**

*To Meg*
*in love*

# Endorsements

"I love learning about revival and this book adds to that hunger. Geoff Waugh, with great integrity and detailed research, draws together much information that will inspire the reader. This is an extension of Geoff's many years of contribution in the area of renewal and revival as editor of the *Renewal Journal*. Geoff has initiated renewal activities in many denominations in Australia and has participated actively as a member in the growth of Gateway Baptist Church in Brisbane."

Rev. Tim Hanna
Senior Pastor
Gateway Baptist Church at Brisbane, Australia

"Geoff Waugh has broken new ground by pulling together evidence of divine impacts on people in revival. He emphasizes the place of prayer and repentance in our response to God's awesome sovereignty and might. This is a book that will inspire you and help you to persist until the earth is 'filled with the knowledge of the glory of the Lord.' "

Dr. Stuart Robinson
Senior Pastor
Crossway Baptist Church at Melbourne, Australia
Author of *Praying the Price* and *Prayer Power*

"I read *Flashpoints of Revival* with much interest and enjoyment. The Rev. Geoff Waugh has offered us a comprehensive account of spiritual renewal over the centuries. Whilst one of the truly great spiritual renewals has occurred in the latter half of the twentieth century, it finds its genesis in the Book of Acts. Amazing signs of God's power and love have occurred in the Christian communities that have been open to revival. Those communities have seen increasing membership. The churches that have closed their minds to charismatic renewal have seen decline in membership. I praise God for the Holy Spirit movement in our time."

> Bishop Ralph E. Wicks
> Anglican Church of Australia

"The Rev. Dr. Geoff Waugh is well able to write about the stories and experiences of revival. He has been a careful and sympathetic student of revival experiences in many parts of the world. In churches that need God's power for great tasks, it is important that God's action in other places be studied. Geoff Waugh has made a crucial contribution to that task."

> Rev. John E. Mavor
> President
> Uniting Church in Australia

"Geoff Waugh's work has a global relevance, which he has applied in the Australian context. As a fellow Australian, I am appreciative. My appreciation is greatly enhanced by a deep respect and affection for the author. He is a competent teacher; an excellent communicator; an informed, disciplined renewalist; and an experienced educator. All these qualities combine to commend the author and his work."

> Rev. Dr. Lewis Born
> Former Moderator
> Queensland Synod of the Uniting Church

"Geoff Waugh places current outpourings of the Holy Spirit in historical context. In 1993 I said that this move of God would go around the world. It has. It is breaking out and touching millions of lives. Geoff's work helps us understand more about God's mighty work in our time."

> Pastor Neil Miers
> President
> Christian Outreach Centre

"This book covers vital information on revival. Geoff Waugh has a deep commitment to revival and teaches on it in our School of Ministries and in many churches. The examples in this book will build your faith and stir revival fire in your heart."

> Pastor David McDonald
> Senior Pastor
> Brisbane Christian Outreach Centre

"Geoff Waugh inspires his students in his degree and diploma courses on the history of revivals. This book covers some of that material and provides an invaluable resource for understanding revivals in history and in current events."

> Pastor Peter C. Earle
> Principal and Associate Pastor
> Brisbane Christian Outreach Centre School of
> Ministries

# Contents

# Foreword

Geoff Waugh and I agree that our generation is likely to be an eyewitness to the greatest outpouring of the Holy Spirit that history has ever known. Many others join us in this expectation, some of them sensing that it will come in the next few years.

Here in America, it seems to me that I have heard more reports of revival-like activity in the past three years than in the previous 30. This has caused revival to be a more frequent topic of Christian conversation than I have ever seen. There is an extraordinary hunger for learning more about how the hand of God works in revival.

That is a major reason why *Flashpoints of Revival* is such a timely book. Christian libraries are well stocked with detailed accounts of certain revivals as well as scholarly analytical histories of revival. But I know of no other book like this one that provides rapid-fire, easy-to-read, factual, literary snapshots of virtually every well-known revival since Pentecost.

As I read this book, I was thrilled to see how God has been so mightily at work in so many different times and places. I felt like I had grasped the overall picture of revival for the first time, and I was moved to pray that God, indeed, would allow me not to be just an observer, but rather a literal participant in the worldwide outpouring that will soon come. As you read this book, I am sure you will be saying the same thing.

C. Peter Wagner
Fuller Theological Seminary
Pasadena, California

# Preface

Bounding across the vivid green ridges and gorges of Papua New Guinea's highlands, I found a gem in Meg, my wonderful wife. We are now grateful grandparents, proud of our extended family, which has grown up during the most momentous explosion of the Church in history. These revival fires that have flared over the years and around the world, along with the possibilities and problems that they bring, are a fascinating and worthwhile study—thus my reason for publishing this book.

My interest in revivals began when I was a young lad. I grew up in a loving family as the son of a Baptist pastor, and my earliest memories include drifting off to sleep under a blanket on the pew while my Mum played the piano in church and listening to the young people sing around our piano in our home at my bedtime. My parents dedicated me to God before I was born, as they did for all their children. (I'm the eldest of nine children—including three after our Mum died and we welcomed a new Mum into our family. All my siblings are now Christians with extended Christian families.) My parents encouraged us to have a love for the Bible and for the heroes of the faith, and I devoured Sunday School books and stories of John Bunyan, John Wesley, John Newton, William Carey, Florence

Nightingale, David Livingstone, Mary Slessor, Hudson Taylor, and scores more.

I'm very thankful for that grounding in evangelical faith, especially in the truth of the Bible, which I believe now more strongly than ever. However, when I later served the Lord as a Baptist minister in Australia and in Papua New Guinea, I soon learned that our way of being the Church carries a lot of cultural baggage. That may be not wrong—just limited. I could see the Church in the Pacific, alive with fresh faith, grappling with cultural and personal transformation, and dealing with the typical challenges of human relationships, which are part of church life in any culture.

Then the opportunity opened for me to work in the Queensland Methodist and the Uniting Church. There I met many compassionate friends who encompassed and encouraged a wide range of views. I am grateful for the experience I gained there, mainly in innovative Christian Education ministries and creative theological college ventures, including studying fearless missiology with Fuller Theological Seminary.

In the 1970's, we encountered—or rather, were encountered by—the wave of renewal and revival. So I started to gather reports on revivals. The church publishers produced a series of my study books, including *Living in the Spirit* and *Church on Fire*, which examine these vibrant, explosive developments.

Our home church, Gateway Baptist in Brisbane, continues to be part of that progressive and tumultuous story. The senior pastors and leadership team guided that church into significant ministries where we saw attendance grow from around 200 to over 1,200 in a decade. We've been pleased to pass on that heritage of dynamic church life to our children, now adults.

Working with various church traditions gave me great scope for renewal ministry. Part of that ministry has been through leading the interdenominational Renewal Fellowship in Brisbane. I deeply appreciate the support and encouragement of that group, especially during our adventures in traveling as teams to various churches and to other countries. I'll always remember the June monsoon rains in Ghana that ceased on the first night of our open-air, combined-churches crusade there and began again the day after our last meeting; teaching inaugural courses on the History of Revivals and on Signs and Wonders at the warmly hospitable Asian Theological Seminary in Manila in the Philippines in their hot summer schools; and trekking to dedicated little churches in the cities and villages of Nepal and Sri Lanka. The bewildering array of faith-filled Bible Schools—ranging from small local church Bible Schools in Nepal and Sri Lanka to the 600-student campus of the indigenous Indian Inland Mission near New Delhi in India—inspired us all.

In 1993 I began editing the interdenominational *Renewal Journal*, collecting testimonies of the marvelous and mysterious work of God around the world. It's published on the Internet at www.pastornet.net.au/renewal with periodical updates. I first gathered much of the material in this book for various journal articles, and I appreciate the staff of Destiny Image Publishers for their suggestions on improving the drafts of that material in this book.

My current teaching position with the innovative Brisbane Christian Outreach Centre School of Ministries (including Distance Education on 100401.57@compuserve.com), a school of Christian Heritage College, helps me further explore the dynamic Pentecostal/Charismatic explosion now transforming individual lives and the life of the Church. I am grateful to the leadership at the Centre and the staff of the School of Ministries for allowing me to be involved with them in fulfilling the mission of the one and only Church of Jesus Christ in the world today.

We are one in Christ and shall be forever. Our perceptions remain limited and partial. We see only the blurred image of the great glory of God, revealed fully in Jesus, who loves us all, gave His life for us all, reigns over us all, and lives in us in His Spirit, the Spirit of God.

The pattern in Jesus' life and ministry and in the early Church is normative for the Church, but we have fallen far short of it. We need to humble ourselves, pray, seek God, and turn from our sin. God promises to hear, forgive, and heal when we do (see 2 Chron. 7:14).

The fire of the Holy Spirit fell on Jesus when He was 30; on Mary, Peter, James, John, and others at Pentecost; on the Samaritans when Peter and John prayed for them; on Saul, the zealous persecutor of Christians, when Ananias prayed for him; and during Peter's preaching in the home of Cornelius. Now countless millions tell the same story. This book gives a few brief glimpses of the Spirit of God touching and transforming their lives. As you read, you can:

A. Ask God to pour out His Spirit in revival (see Mt. 7:7).

B. Believe Him (see Jn. 20:27-29).

C. Commit yourself to Him (see Ps. 37:5).

Have faith in God. He has promised to pour out His Spirit on all people. Our faith is not in our faith; it wavers. Our faith is not in our commitment, our gifts, or our prayers; they express our response to God. Our faith is in our God.

This account of flashpoints of revival is partial and incomplete. Much more can, and will, be told. I am grateful to God for His great grace and mercy as shown in the story of revivals. My prayer is that you will be part of that story.

# Introduction

We drove for over an hour in torrential rain for our first evening open-air crusade meeting in Ghana, West Africa. As the guest speaker, on my first visit to Africa, I wondered why the meetings had not been switched from the market area to a church building with a roof. Our hosts from a small independent church that was cooperating with other local churches for these meetings explained that they always held crusade meetings outside in the market area where the people were. *But what about the rain?* I wondered.

Immediately, before this visit to Ghana, I taught a course on "signs and wonders" at the Asian Theological Seminary in Manila in the Philippines. (It was during my mid-year vacation from the Brisbane Christian Outreach Centre School of Ministries where I teach.) While teaching the class, I never dreamed that I and several other Australians would be holding outdoor meetings in the middle of the tropical monsoon rains in equatorial Africa! But there we were. Now, we really needed some kind of "sign," and I was certainly "wondering."

In their class seminars, my students in Manila had reported on various signs and wonders that they had experienced in their churches. Most of them expected God to do the same things in their churches as He did in the New Testament. One student, a part-time Baptist pastor and a police inspector, had interviewed—interrogated—a Pentecostal pastor about miraculous answers to prayer in their church. That student reported to the class how the Pentecostal church had sent a team of young people to the local mental hospital for a monthly meeting where they sang and witnessed and prayed for people. Over 40 patients had attended their first meeting there, and they prayed for 26 personally. A month later, when they returned for their next meeting, all 26 had been discharged and sent home.

What would happen in Africa? I didn't know. When we arrived at the mountain town of Suhum, it was dark. The torrential rain had cut off the electricity supply. The rain eased off a bit, so we gathered in the market area and prayed for God to guide us and to take over. Soon the rain ceased. The electricity came on. The host team began excitedly shouting that it was a miracle. "We will talk about this for years," they exclaimed with gleaming eyes.

I asked them again why they had planned outdoor meetings in the rainy season. They told me that if I could only come at that time, then they trusted God to work it all out. Soon the musicians from one of the local churches had plugged in their instruments to the sound system. I noticed that the loudspeakers were not facing the faithful Christians gathered in the fluorescent-lit open area, but were pointed at the surrounding houses, the stores, and the hotel.

My interpreter that night didn't know much English. I think he preached his own sermon based on some phrases of mine he understood or guessed, and apparently he did well. When we invited people to respond and give their lives to Christ, they came from the surrounding darkness into the light. Some wandered over from the pub, smelling of beer. They kept the ministry team busy praying and arranging follow-up with local churches.

At that point I left the work to the locals who understood one another. I just moved about laying hands on people's heads and praying for them, as did many others. People reported various touches of God in their lives. Some were healed. Later that week an older man excitedly told how he had come to the meeting almost blind but now he could see.

Each day we held the morning worship and teaching sessions for Christians in a church, which became quite hot under an iron roof on sunny days. On the third morning I vividly "saw" great light fill the church and swallow up or remove blackness. At that point the African Christians became very noisy, vigorously celebrating and shouting praises to God. A fresh anointing seemed to fall on them just then.

Although it didn't rain the whole time we were holding meetings, the day after our meetings finished, the rains began again. The following week we saw floods in Ghana reported on international television. Later on we received letters telling us how the church where we held our morning meetings had grown, expanded their building, and had sent out teams of committed young people in evangelism! Through that experience, God showed us a glimpse of what He is doing in a big way in the earth right now.

## What Is Revival?

Millions of people believe in Jesus today. He is alive and well. He changes those who give their lives to Him. People who once ignored Him now live for Him. Many who only knew His name as a swear word or as a religious chant now love Him.

This change happens when people believe in God. God gives His Spirit, the Spirit of Jesus, to His people. God empowers His people by His Spirit. That's what He did in Israel's history, in Jesus' life, in the early Church, and through the centuries till now. And He still does.

The Spirit of God may come suddenly and powerfully as at Sinai with Moses, at the dedication of the temple in Jerusalem with Solomon, at Pentecost with the early Church, and at the home of Cornelius, the Roman centurion. Sometimes the Spirit of the Lord comes upon individuals, who then spark a powerful move of God's Spirit among the people. Such visitations of God's Spirit often cause revival, and those revivals bring profound change. Thousands become Christians. Crime rates drop. Justice and righteousness prevail.

Millions of Christians now pray earnestly for such a revival. Selwyn Hughes notes:

> In all the years that I have been a Christian I have never witnessed such a burden and expectancy for revival as I do at this moment among the true people of God. Wherever I go I meet prayerful Christians whose spirit witnesses with my own that a mighty Holy Spirit revival is on the way. The 1960s and 1970s were characterized by the word "renewal". Then in the eighties, the word began slowly losing currency, and another appeared to take its place—revival. And why? Because great and wonderful though renewal is, many are beginning to see that there are greater things in our Father's storehouse, and slowly but surely their faith is rising to a flash point (Hughes 1990, 7).

Revival is not welcomed by everyone, however, because it involves humility, awareness of our unworthiness, confession of sin, repentance, restitution, seeking and offering forgiveness, and following Christ wholeheartedly. It then impacts society with conviction, godliness, justice, peace, and righteousness. Some people do not want that, especially if revival is accompanied by people being overwhelmed, which often happens.

One of the best explanations of revival that I have found is from Arthur Wallis, in his classic book, *In the Day of Thy Power*. Wallis observes:

> Numerous writings...confirm that revival is divine intervention in the normal course of spiritual things. It is God revealing

Himself to man in awesome holiness and irresistible power. It is such a manifest working of God that human personalities are overshadowed and human programs abandoned. It is man retiring into the background because God has taken the field. It is the Lord…working in extraordinary power on saint and sinner. … Revival must of necessity make an impact on the community and this is one means by which we may distinguish it from the more usual operations of the Holy Spirit (Wallis 1956, 20, 23).

Edwin Orr, historian of revivals, distinguishes between *revivals*, which primarily affect churches and their surrounding community, and wide-scale *awakenings*, which affect the whole of society. According to Orr:

A spiritual awakening is a movement of the Holy Spirit bringing about a revival of New Testament Christianity in the Church of Christ and its related community. … It accomplishes the reviving of the Church, the awakening of the masses and the movements of uninstructed people toward the Christian faith; the revived church by many or few is moved to engage in evangelism, teaching and social action (Orr 1973, vii-viii).

As individuals and churches are renewed, they prepare the way for revival in the land. A spiritual awakening touches the community when God's Spirit moves in power, and often this awakening begins in people who are earnestly praying for and expecting revival. "Will You not revive us again, that Your people may rejoice in You?" (Ps. 85:6 NKJ)

### Revival in the Old Testament

Many times in the long history of Israel, the Spirit of the Lord moved upon that nation. The best known Bible verse on revival is God's promise to answer the prayers of His repentant people. It comes in the chapter that tells how the glory of the Lord filled the temple. God gave that promise at the dedication of the temple in Jerusalem: "If My people who are called by My name will humble themselves, and pray and seek My face, and turn from their wicked ways, then I will hear from heaven, and will forgive their sin and heal their land" (2 Chron. 7:14 NKJ).

He kept His promise, and He still does. The history of Israel gives many examples. Wilbur Smith listed seven revivals in the Old Testament in addition to the one under Jonah. These revivals involved:

1. Jacob's household (see Gen. 35:1-15).

2. Asa (see 2 Chron. 15:1-15).

3. Joash (see 2 Kings 11-12; 2 Chron. 23-24).

4. Hezekiah (see 2 Kings 18:1-8; 2 Chron. 29-31).

5. Josiah (see 2 Kings 22-23; 2 Chron. 34-35).

6. Haggai and Zechariah with Zerubbabel (see Ezra 5-6).

7. Ezra with Nehemiah (see Neh. 9:1-6; 12:44-47).

He noted nine characteristics of these revivals:

1. They occurred in times of moral darkness and national depression.

2. Each began in the heart of a consecrated servant of God who became the energizing power behind it.

3. Each revival rested on the Word of God, and most were the result of proclaiming God's Word with power.

4. All resulted in a return to the worship of God.

5. Each witnessed the destruction of idols where they existed.

6. In each revival, there was a recorded separation from sin.

7. In every revival, the people returned to obeying God's laws.

8. There was a restoration of great joy and gladness.

9. Each revival was followed by a period of national prosperity (Pratney 1994, 13).

Those characteristics of revival have continued through the history of God's people. They still happen in revivals all over the world.

## Revival in the New Testament

Jesus emphasized these same principles of obeying God and living under God's reign. He called people to repentance and wholehearted commitment to God in the power of the Holy Spirit. He announced and demonstrated the kingdom of God in everything, not just in religious activities.

The Spirit of the Lord came upon Jesus at His baptism. He then ministered in the power of the Spirit. That kind of ministry is typical of outpourings of the Spirit in the Church. Jesus ushered in the new era of the new covenant written in His blood. Through the cross and the resurrection, Jesus conquered evil. So, every revival stems from the cross and demonstrates the power of the risen Lord in those who give their lives to Him.

The early Church lived in continuous revival. It saw rapid growth of the Church by the power of the Holy Spirit from the initial outburst at Pentecost, which saved 3,000 people. Multitudes joined the Church, amid turmoil and persecution.

Those early Christians lived in the power of the Spirit. They were not faultless, but they were on fire. Observers described them as people who "turned the world upside down" (Acts 17:6).

The Book of Acts tells the amazing story of the rapid growth of the early Church. Here's a brief summary of the events recorded in Acts:

1. At Pentecost about 3,000 were added to them (see Acts 2:41).

2. Later, many who heard the word believed, about 5,000 (see Acts 4:4).

3. More believers were added to the Lord, great numbers of both men and women (see Acts 5:14).

4. The number of the disciples increased greatly in Jerusalem, and a great many of the priests became obedient to the faith (see Acts 6:7).

5. The Church throughout Judea, Galilee, and Samaria had peace and was built up. Living in the fear of the Lord and in the comfort of the Holy Spirit, it increased in numbers (see Acts 9:31).

6. The Lord's hand was on them at Antioch and a great number became believers (see Acts 11:21).

7. Many people were brought to the Lord through Barnabas (see Acts 11:24).

8. The word of the Lord continued to advance and multiply (see Acts 12:24).

9. The churches increased in numbers daily (see Acts 16:5).

The Lord did that through His Spirit in His people. It's an astounding account. Imagine it happening in your area! That is exactly what is happening now in many places around the world.

As with Pentecost, revivals are often unexpected, sudden, and revolutionary, and they impact large numbers of people, bringing them to repentance and faith in Jesus the Lord. The day of Pentecost demonstrated these vital principles of revival:

A. **God's Sovereignty**: "*When the day of Pentecost was fully come*" (Acts 2:1). God chose the time, the day, the place, and the people. His Spirit came suddenly at the Pentecost festival in Jerusalem upon a praying group, and people were overwhelmed. Revival is often like that.

B. **Prayer**: "*Constantly in prayer, in one place*" (see Acts 1:14; 2:1). The believers gathered together to pray and wait on God. Those followers of Jesus had been praying earnestly for over a month after Jesus' arrest, torture, execution, and then His miraculous reappearance. All revivals are born and flourish among praying people.

C. **Unity**: "*With one accord*" (Acts 2:1). They met in unity with love and humility. Every revival sweeps across our barriers and differences. Revival brings amazing unity among God's people.

D. **Obedience to the Spirit**: "*The Spirit gave them utterance*" (Acts 2:4). Filled with the Spirit, they began using gifts of the Spirit. In all revivals the Spirit of God moves upon the people just as in the early Church. People rediscover the empowering Presence of the Spirit and are sometimes surprised at the gifts the Holy Spirit gives them.

E. **Preaching**: "*Heed my words*" (Acts 2:14 NKJ). Peter preached with anointed boldness. So have thousands of God's servants ever since, especially in revival—in churches, in halls, in the open fields, in underground house churches, or in vast crusades. Anointed preaching is happening today more than ever.

F. **Repentance**: "*What shall we do? ...Repent ...*" (Acts 2:37-38). Large numbers repented. The Holy Spirit convicts people, especially through powerful preaching and praying; we realize how far we have fallen from what we should be. Revival produces repentance on a massive scale.

G. **Evangelism**: "*Three thousand souls were added to them*" (Acts 2:41 NKJ). As the believers witnessed through the power of the Spirit, thousands were saved. In the early Church this happened daily (see Acts 2:47). Revivals produce that kind of zeal in witnessing about the great things God has done.

**Summary of Revivals in Church History (A.D. 100–1600)**

Throughout history many people led reform and revival movements, especially when faith sunk low and formalism set in. Those movements powerfully affected the Church and the community.

From the second century into the fifth century, the Montanists flourished in Asia Minor. The leader of this group, Montanus, spoke in tongues at his baptism and began prophesying. His movement called people to holy living, and they expected the Lord to return soon. They valued the gifts of the Spirit, especially prophecy. The lawyer-theologian, Tertullian, joined the movement early in the third century and challenged the worldliness of the Church of his day.

Beginning in the fourth century, various church leaders founded monastic orders devoted to the service of God and people. In the fifth century Augustine of Hippo in North Africa strongly influenced the Church and society through his writings, and Patrick told of the conversions of thousands of the Irish, initiating active Celtic missionary activity.

By A.D. 600 Augustine of Canterbury and his missionaries saw thousands accept Christianity in England, and it was reported that they imitated the powers of the apostles in the signs that they displayed.

In the twelfth century Peter Waldo and the Waldensians began reform and revival movements that challenged the church and impacted society.

In the thirteenth century Francis of Assisi called people to forsake all and follow Jesus. Many did, and they influenced others in society.

John Wycliffe and his itinerant preachers, the Lollards, made a powerful impact on England in the fourteenth century. They aroused strong opposition leading to many martyrdoms.

In the fifteenth century John Huss in Bohemia and Girolamo Savonarola in Italy led strong reform movements that brought revival but led to their martyrdoms. Huss was known for his un-blemished purity of life and uncompromising stand for truth in a decadent society. Savonarola fasted, prayed, and preached with prophetic fire, which confronted evils of his time, filled the churches, and brought honesty into much of civic and business life.

Gutenberg's printing press, invented in 1456, made the Scriptures widely available. This helped spark the sixteenth-century Reformation with leaders such as Martin Luther in Germany proclaiming justification by faith alone based on the supreme authority of Scripture; John Calvin in Geneva empha-sizing the awesome sovereignty and grace of God; and Huldreich Zwingli in Switzerland initially calling for freedom of conscience, though later denying this for others. Radical re-formers, such as Felix Manz, the first Anabaptist martyr, some-times were killed in those days of heated religious conflict. John Knox fearlessly called Scotland to repentance amid the intense political and religious zeal of the times.

Revival movements have won thousands of people to faith in Jesus Christ and have made a powerful impact on society. And they still happen today! Using many eyewitness accounts, this book tells a little of that story from the Great Awakening of the eighteenth century to revivals today.

# Chapter One

# Eighteenth Century

## 1727

### *August 13—Herrnhut, Germany (Nicholas von Zinzendorf)*

No one present could tell exactly what happened on that Wednesday morning at the specially called communion service. The fire of God fell, and the glory of the Lord came upon several hundred refugees so powerfully that they hardly knew if they were on earth or in Heaven. One of them described the experience by writing:

[Church history] abounds in records of special outpourings of the Holy Ghost, and verily the thirteenth of August, 1727, was a day of the outpouring of the Holy Spirit. We saw the hand of God and His wonders, and we were all under the cloud of our fathers baptized with their Spirit. The Holy Ghost came upon us and in those days great signs and wonders took place in our midst. From that time scarcely a day passed but what we beheld His almighty workings amongst us. A great hunger after the Word of God took possession of us so that we had to have three services every day, viz. 5.0 and 7:30 am and 9.0 pm. Every one desired above everything else that the Holy Spirit might have full control. Self-love and self-will, as well as all disobedience, disappeared and an overwhelming flood of grace swept us all out into the great ocean of Divine Love (Greenfield 1927, 14).

The young leader of that community, Count Nicholas Ludwig of Zinzendorf, gave this account many years later:

> We needed to come to the Communion with a sense of the loving nearness of the Saviour. This was the great comfort which has made this day a generation ago to be a festival, because on this day twenty-seven years ago the Congregation of Herrnhut, assembled for communion (at the Berthelsdorf church) were all dissatisfied with themselves. They had quit judging each other because they had become convinced, each one, of his lack of worth in the sight of God and each felt himself at this Communion to be in view of the noble countenance of the Saviour....
>
> In this view of the man of sorrows and acquainted with grief, their hearts told them that He would be their patron and their priest who was at once changing their tears into oil of gladness and their misery into happiness. This firm confidence changed them in a single moment into a happy people which they are to this day, and into their happiness they have since led many thousands of others through the memory and help which the heavenly grace once given to themselves, so many thousand times confirmed to them since then (Greenfield 1927, 15).

Zinzendorf described the experience as "a sense of the nearness of Christ" given to everyone present, and also to others of their community who were working elsewhere at the time.

So who was this group of believers who had assembled in Herrnhut? And how did this powerful move of God's Spirit come about?

The group at Herrnhut was mostly made up of Moravian refugees. The Moravian brethren had grown from the work and martyrdom of the Bohemian reformer, John Huss. They suffered centuries of persecution, and many had been killed, imprisoned, tortured, or banished from their homeland. Seeking refuge, this group had fled to Germany where the young

Christian nobleman, Count Zinzendorf, offered them asylum on his estates in Saxony in 1722. They named their new home, *Herrnhut*, which means "the Lord's Watch."

The Moravians were the first group to make their homes there, but soon other persecuted Christians were attracted to Herrnhut as well—including Lutherans, Reformed, and Anabaptists. By early 1727, heated controversies threatened to disrupt the community. The various sects had become deeply divided and critical of one another, arguing over issues such as predestination, holiness, and baptism.

The young German nobleman, Count Zinzendorf, pleaded for unity, love, and repentance. Converted in early childhood at four years of age, Zinzendorf composed and signed a covenant: "Dear Saviour, be mine, and I will be Thine." His life motto was, "Jesus only," and he had learned the secret of prevailing prayer. As a teenager he actively established prayer groups, and on finishing college at Halle at 16, he gave the famous Professor Francke a list of seven praying societies he had established.

At Herrnhut, Zinzendorf visited all the adult members of the deeply divided community. He drew up a covenant calling upon them to seek out and emphasize the points in which they agreed rather than stressing their differences.

On May 12, 1727, they all signed an agreement to dedicate their lives, as he dedicated his, to the service of the Lord Jesus Christ. A spirit of grace, unity, and supplications grew among them. The Moravian revival of 1727 was thus preceded and then sustained by extraordinary praying.

On July 16, Zinzendorf poured out his soul in prayer accompanied with a flood of tears. This prayer produced an extraordinary effect. The whole community began praying as never before.

On July 22, many members of the community covenanted together of their own accord to meet often to pour out their hearts in prayer and hymns.

On August 5, after a large prayer meeting at midnight where great emotion prevailed, Zinzendorf spent the whole night in prayer with approximately 12 or 14 others.

On Sunday, August 10, Pastor Rothe, while leading the service at Herrnhut, was overwhelmed by the power of the Lord about noon. He sank down into the dust before God. So did the whole congregation. They continued until midnight in prayer and singing, weeping and praying.

*On Wednesday, August 13, the Holy Spirit was poured out on them all.* Their prayers were answered in ways far beyond anyone's expectations. Many of them decided to set aside certain times for continued earnest prayer. Zinzendorf observed: "The Saviour permitted to come upon us a Spirit of whom we had hitherto not had any experience or knowledge. ... Hitherto we had been the leaders and helpers. Now the Holy Spirit Himself took full control of everything and everybody" (Greenfield 1927, 21).

On Tuesday, August 26, 24 men and 24 women covenanted together to continue praying in intervals of one hour each, day and night, each hour allocated by lots to different people.

On Wednesday, August 27, this new commitment to intercession began. Others joined these intercessors, and the number involved increased to 77. They all carefully observed the hour that had been appointed to them and met weekly to discuss prayer needs.

The children began a similar plan among themselves, and adults who heard their infant supplications were deeply moved. The children's prayers and supplications had a powerful effect on the whole community.

The astonishing prayer meeting that began in 1727 lasted 100 years. It was unique. Known as the Hourly Intercession, it involved relays of men and women in prayer to God without ceasing. That prayer also led to action, especially evangelism. After their baptism of fire, this group became pioneering evangelists and missionaries, using the missionary zeal that began with the outpouring of the Holy Spirit. Many missionaries left that village community in the next 25 years, all constantly supported in prayer.

Fifty years later, before the beginning of modern missions with William Carey, the Moravian Church had already sent out more than 100 missionaries. Their English missionary magazine, *Periodical Accounts*, inspired William Carey. He threw a copy of the paper on a table at a Baptist meeting, saying, "See what the Moravians have done! Cannot we follow their example and in obedience to our Heavenly Master go out into the world, and preach the Gospel to the heathen?" (Greenfield 1927, 19).

Prayer precedes Pentecost. The believers at Herrnhut learned this lesson well and demonstrated the importance of prayer to future generations. Another one of the major results of their baptism in the Holy Spirit was a joyful assurance of their pardon and salvation. This made a strong impact on people in many countries, including the Wesleys, and profoundly affected the eighteenth-century evangelical awakening.

## 1735

### *January—New England, America (Jonathan Edwards)*

Jonathan Edwards, the preacher and scholar who later became a President of Princeton College, was a prominent leader in a revival movement that came to be called the Great Awakening as it spread through the communities of New England and the pioneer settlements in America. From late December 1734 into 1735 an unusually powerful move of God's Spirit brought revival to Northampton and then spread through New England in the northeast of America. Converts to Christianity reached 50,000 out of a total of 250,000 colonists.

This revival radically altered people's lives. Edwards noted that:

a great and earnest concern about the great things of religion and the eternal world, became *universal* in all parts of the town, and among persons of all degrees and all ages; the noise among the *dry bones* waxed louder and louder; all other talk but about spiritual and eternal things, was soon thrown by....

The minds of people were wonderfully taken off from the *world*; it was treated among us as a thing of very little consequence. They seemed to follow their worldly business, more as a part of their duty, than from any disposition they had to it....

And the work of *conversion* was carried on in a most *astonishing* manner, and increased more and more; souls did as it were come by flocks to Jesus Christ. From day to day, for many months together, might be seen evident instances of sinners *brought out of darkness into marvellous light*...with *a new song of praise to God in their mouths*....

Our public assemblies were then beautiful: the congregation was *alive* in God's service, every one earnestly intent on the public worship, every *hearer* eager to drink in the words of the *minister* as they came from his mouth; the assembly in general were, from time to time, *in tears* while the word was preached; *some* weeping with sorrow and distress, *others* with joy and love, *others* with pity and concern for the souls of their neighbours....

Those amongst us who had been *formerly converted*, were greatly enlivened, and renewed with fresh and extraordinary incomes of the Spirit of God; though some much more than others, *according to the measure of the gift of Christ*. Many who before had laboured under *difficulties* about their own state, had now their *doubts* removed by more satisfying experience, and more clear discoveries of God's love (Edwards 1835, 348).

Describing the characteristics of the revival, Edwards said that it gave people:

An extraordinary sense of the awful majesty, greatness and *holiness of God*, so as sometimes to overwhelm soul and body; a sense of the piercing, all seeing eye of God, so as sometimes to take away the bodily strength; and an extraordinary view of the infinite terribleness of the *wrath of God*, together with a sense of the ineffable misery of sinners exposed to this wrath. ... and ...

longings after more love to Christ, and greater conformity to him; especially longing after these two things, to be more perfect in *humility* and *adoration*. The flesh and the heart seem often to cry out, lying low before God and adoring him with greater love and humility. ... The person felt a great delight in singing praises to God and Jesus Christ, and longing that this present life may be as it were one continued song of praise to God. ... Together with living by faith to a great degree, there was a constant and extraordinary distrust of our own strength and wisdom; a great dependence on God for his help ... and being restrained from the most horrid sins (Edwards 1835, 377).

In 1735, when the New England revival was strong, George Whitefield in England and Howell Harris in Wales were converted. Both were 21 and both ignited revival fires, seeing thousands converted and communities changed. By 1736 Harris began forming his converts into societies, and by 1739 there were nearly 30 such societies. Whitefield journeyed extensively, visiting Georgia in 1738 (the first of seven journeys to America), then ministered powerfully with Howell Harris in Wales in 1739 and with Jonathan Edwards in New England in 1740, all while in his early twenties.

Around that same time, another man who would soon help spread revival was on his way to America. At the end of 1735, John Wesley sailed to Georgia, an American colony, as an Anglican missionary. A company of Moravian immigrants sailed on that same vessel, and during a terrible storm they all faced the danger of shipwreck. John Wesley wrote about this experience in his journal on Sunday, January 25, 1736:

> At seven I went to the Germans. I had long before observed the great seriousness of their behaviour. Of their humility they had given a continual proof by performing those servile offices for the other passengers which none of the English would undertake; for which they desired and would receive no pay, saying, "It was good for their proud hearts," and "their loving Saviour had done more for them." And every day had given them occasion of showing a meekness, which no injury could move. If they were pushed, struck or thrown down, they rose again and went away; but no complaint was found in their mouth. Here was now an opportunity of trying whether they were delivered from the spirit of fear, as well as from that of pride, anger and revenge. In the midst of the Psalm wherewith their service began, the sea broke over, split the main-sail in pieces, covered the ship and poured in between the decks, as if the great deep had already swallowed us up. A terrible screaming began among the English. The Germans calmly sung on. I asked one of them afterwards: "Were you not afraid?" He answered, "I thank God, no." I asked: "But were not your women and children afraid?" He replied mildly: "No, our women and children are not afraid to die" (Greenfield 1927, 35-36).

Back in England in 1738, after his return from a brief and frustrating missionary career in Georgia, John and his brother Charles were challenged by the Moravian missionary, Peter Bohler. In March 1738, John Wesley wrote:

> Saturday, 4 March—I found my brother at Oxford, recovering from his pleurisy; and with him Peter Bohler, by whom (in the hand of the great God) I was, on Sunday the 5th, clearly convinced of unbelief, of the want of that faith whereby alone we are saved. Immediately it struck into my mind, "Leave off preaching. How can you preach to others, who have not faith yourself?" I asked Bohler whether he thought I should leave it off or not. He answered, "By no means." I asked, "But what

can I preach?" He said, "Preach faith *till* you have it; and then, *because* you have it, you *will* preach faith."

Monday, 6 March—I began preaching this new doctrine, though my soul started back from the work. The first person to whom I offered salvation by faith alone was a prisoner under sentence of death. His name was Clifford. Peter Bohler had many times desired me to speak to him before. But I could not prevail on myself so to do; being still a zealous assertor of the impossibility of a death-bed repentance (Idle 1986, 43).

Both John and Charles were converted in May 1738, Charles first, and John three days later on Wednesday, May 24. He wrote his famous testimony in his journal:

In the evening I went very unwillingly to a society in Aldersgate Street, where one was reading Luther's preface to the *Epistle to the Romans*. About a quarter before nine, while he was describing the change which God works in the heart through faith in Christ, I felt my heart strangely warmed. I felt I did trust in Christ, Christ alone, for salvation; and an assurance was given me, that he had taken away my sins, even mine, and saved me from the law of sin and death (Idle 1986, 46).

Later that year John Wesley visited the Moravian community at Herrnhut. He admired their zeal and love for the Lord, and he prayed that their kind of Christianity, full of the Holy Spirit, would spread through the earth. Back in England he preached evangelically, gathered converts into religious societies (which were nicknamed Methodists because of his methodical procedures), and continued to relate warmly with the Moravians. Evangelical revival fires began to stir in England and burst into flame the following year.

## 1739

### *January 1—London (George Whitefield, John Wesley)*

During 1739 there was an astonishing expansion of revival in England. On January 1, the Wesleys and Whitefield (recently back from America) and four others from their former Holy

Club at Oxford University, along with 60 others, met in London for prayer and a love feast. The Spirit of God moved powerfully on them all. Many fell down, overwhelmed. The meeting went all night, and they realized they had been empowered in a fresh visitation from God.

John Wesley gave the following account:

> Mr. Hall, Kinchin, Ingham, Whitefield, Hitchins, and my brother Charles were present at our lovefeast in Fetter Lane, with about sixty of our brethren. About three in the morning, as we were continuing instant in prayer, the power of God came mightily upon us, insomuch that many cried out for exceeding joy, and many fell to the ground. As soon as we were recovered a little from that awe and amazement at the presence of his majesty, we broke out with one voice, "We praise Thee, O God, we acknowledge Thee to be the Lord" (Idle 1986, 55).

This Pentecost on New Year's Day launched the evangelical revival in England which became part of the Great Awakening. Revival spread rapidly.

In February 1739, Whitefield started preaching to the Kingswood coal miners in the open fields near Bristol. He preached outside because many churches opposed him, accusing him and other evangelicals of "enthusiasm." When he started the meetings in February, about 200 attended. By March, 20,000 attended.

Whitefield invited John Wesley to take over. Wesley reluctantly agreed and began his famous open-air preaching, which continued for 50 years. He later described that first weekend in his journal:

> Saturday, 31 March—In the evening I reached Bristol, and met Mr. Whitefield. I could scarce reconcile myself at first to this strange way of preaching in the fields, of which he set me an example on Sunday; having been all my life (till very lately) so tenacious of every point relating to decency and

order, that I should have thought the saving of souls almost a sin if it had not been done in a church.

Sunday, 1 April—In the evening, I begun expounding our Lord's Sermon on the Mount (one pretty remarkable precedent of field-preaching) to a little society in Nicholas Street.

Monday, 2 April—At four in the afternoon I submitted to be more vile, and proclaimed in the highways the glad tidings of salvation, speaking from a little eminence in a ground adjoining to the city, to almost three thousand people. The scripture on which I spoke was "The Spirit of the Lord is upon me, because he has anointed me to preach the gospel to the poor" (Idle 1986, 56-57).

Sometimes strange manifestations accompanied revival preaching. Wesley wrote in his journal on April 26, 1739, that during his preaching at Newgate, Bristol, "One, and another, and another sunk to the earth; they dropped on every side as thunderstruck" (Backhouse 1996, 212).

He returned to London in June reporting on the amazing move of God's Spirit with many conversions and many people falling prostrate under God's power—a phenomenon that he never encouraged! Features of this revival were enthusiastic singing, powerful preaching, and the gathering of converts into small societies called weekly Class Meetings.

Initially, leaders such as George Whitefield criticized some manifestations in Wesley's meetings, but this changed. Wesley wrote on July 7, 1739:

I had opportunity to talk with Mr. Whitefield about those outward signs which had so often accompanied the inward work of God. I found his objections were chiefly grounded on gross misrepresentations of matter of fact. But the next day he had opportunity of informing himself better: for no sooner had he begun (in the application of his sermon) to invite all sinners to believe in Christ, than four persons sank down, close to him, almost in the same moment. One of them lay without either sense or motion; a second trembled exceedingly; the third had strong convulsions all over his body, but made no noise, unless by groans; the fourth, equally convulsed, called upon God, with strong cries and tears. From this time, I trust, we shall all suffer God to carry on His own work in the way that pleaseth Him (Backhouse 1996, 212).

Both John Wesley and George Whitefield continued preaching outdoors as well as in churches that welcomed them. Whitefield's seven visits to America continued to fan the flames of revival there.

Revival caught fire in Scotland also. After returning from America in 1741, Whitefield visited Glasgow. Two ministers in villages nearby invited him to return in 1742 because revival had already begun in their area. Conversions and prayer groups multiplied. Whitefield preached there at Cambuslang about four miles from Glasgow. During the opening meetings on a Sunday, Whitefield saw the great crowds on the hillside gripped with conviction, repentance, and weeping more than he had seen elsewhere. The next weekend 20,000 gathered on Saturday and up to 50,000 on Sunday for the quarterly communion. The visit was charged with Pentecostal power that even amazed Whitefield.

## 1745

### *August 8—Crossweeksung, America (David Brainerd)*

David Brainerd, a missionary to the North American Indians from 1743 until his death at age 29 in 1747, tells of the revival that broke out among the Indians at Crossweeksung on August 8, 1745. The power of God seemed to come like a rushing mighty wind, and the Indians were overwhelmed by God.

Brainerd emphasized the compassion of the Lord, the provisions of the gospel, and the free offer of divine grace. The people's response was amazing. Idolatry was abandoned, marriages repaired, drunkenness practically disappeared, and honesty and repayments of debts prevailed. Money once wasted on excessive drinking was used for family and communal needs. Their communities were filled with love.

Part of his journal for Thursday, August 8, 1745, says that

the power of God seemed to descend on the assembly "like a rushing mighty wind" and with an astonishing energy bore all down before it. I stood amazed at the influence that seized the audience almost universally and could compare it to nothing more aptly than the irresistible force of a mighty torrent.... Almost all persons of all ages were bowed down with concern together, and scarce one was able to withstand the shock of this suprising operation (Howard 1949, 216-217)

On November 20, he described the revival at Crossweeksung in his general comments about that year (during which he had ridden his horse more than 3,000 miles to reach Indian tribes in New England):

I might now justly make many remarks on a work of grace so very remarkable as this has been in divers respects; but shall confine myself to a few general hints only.

1. It is remarkable that God began this work among the Indians at a time when I had least hope and, to my apprehension, the least rational prospect of seeing a work of grace propagated amongst them....

2. It is remarkable how God providentially, and in a manner almost unaccountable, called these Indians together to be instructed in the great things that concerned their souls; how He seized their minds with the most solemn and weighty concern for their eternal salvation, as fast as they came to the place where His Word was preached....

3. It is likewise remarkable how God preserved these poor ignorant Indians from being prejudiced against me and the truths I taught them....

4. Nor is it less wonderful how God was pleased to provide a remedy for my want of skill and freedom in the Indian language

by remarkably fitting my interpreter for, and assisting him in, the performance of his work....

5. It is further remarkable that God has carried on His work here by such means, and in such manner, as tended to obviate and leave no room for those prejudices and objections that have often been raised against such a work...[because] this great awakening, this surprising concern, was never excited by any harangues of terror, but always appeared most remarkable when I insisted upon the *compassions of a dying Saviour*, the *plentiful provisions of the gospel*, and the *free offers of divine grace to needy distressed sinners*.

6. The effects of this work have likewise been very remarkable. ... Their pagan notions and idolatrous practices seem to be entirely abandoned in these parts. They are regulated and appear regularly disposed in the affairs of marriage. They seem generally divorced from drunkenness...although before it was common for some or other of them to be drunk almost every day. ... A principle of honesty and justice appears in many of them, and they seem concerned to discharge their old debts. ... Their manner of living is much more decent and comfortable than formerly, having now the benefit of that money which they used to consume upon strong drink. Love seems to reign among them, especially those who have given evidence of a saving change (Howard 1949, 239-251).

## 1781

### *December 25—Cornwall, England*

Forty years after the Great Awakening began, the fires of revival had died out in many places. Concerned leaders called the church to pray.

Jonathan Edwards in America had written a treatise called, *A Humble Attempt to Promote Explicit Agreement and Visible Union of God's People in Extra-ordinary Prayer for the Revival of Religion and the Advancement of Christ's Kingdom.* It was reprinted in both England and Scotland and was circulated widely.

John Erskine of Edinburgh persisted in urging prayer for revival through extensive correspondence around the world. He instigated widespread combined churches' monthly prayer meetings for revival, called Concerts of Prayer.

Prayer groups for revival multiplied across Great Britian and America. For example, intercessors prayed early on Christmas morning, Tuesday, December 25, 1781, at St. Just Church in Cornwall from 3 a.m. until 9 a.m. and again on Christmas evening because the Spirit of God moved so strongly on them. They continued praying together through January and February, and by March, 1782, they were praying regularly until midnight. Hundreds were converted at these prayer meetings. Revival stirred England again. Baptists, Methodists, and Anglicans joined together with others in these prayer meetings for revival.

John Wesley, then 83, visited the area in 1784 and wrote, "This country is all on fire and the flame is spreading from village to village" (Robinson 1992, 8).

The chapel originally built by George Whitefield in Tottenham Court Road in London was enlarged to seat 5,000 people and so became the largest church building in the world at that time.

Once again praying people and powerful preaching stirred England and North America, bringing a renewed emphasis on conversion and righteousness.

That eighteenth-century revival of holiness brought about a spiritual awakening in England and America. By the end of the century, the Methodists were established with 140,000 members, and other churches and Christians were being renewed.

It impacted England with social change and created the climate for political reform such as the abolition of slavery through the work of William Wilberforce, William Buxton, and others. John Howard and Elizabeth Fry led prison reform. Florence Nightingale founded modern nursing. Ashley Cooper, the Earl of Shaftesbury, reformed employment conditions.

The movement grew. William Carey, Andrew Fuller, John Sutcliffe, and other leaders began the Union of Prayer, calling Christians to pray together regularly for revival. By 1792, the year after John Wesley died, this Second Great Awakening (1792-1830) began to sweep Great Britain and America.

# Chapter Two

# Nineteenth Century

## 1800

### *June-July—Red and Gasper Rivers, America (James McGready)*

James McGready, a Presbyterian minister in Kentucky, promoted a "concert of prayer" every first Monday of the month and urged his people to pray for him at sunset on Saturday evening and sunrise Sunday morning. And, in the summer of 1800, revival swept Kentucky.

McGready had three small congregations in Muddy River, Red River, and Gasper River in Logan County in the southwest of the state. Most of these people, who were refugees from all states in the Union, had fled from justice or punishment. They included murderers, horse thieves, highway robbers, and counterfeiters. The area was nicknamed Rogues Harbor.

Four- to five-hundred people from McGready's three congregations gathered with five ministers at Red River for a "camp meeting" in June 1800. On the last day of their meetings, God's Spirit fell on them with mighty power. People fell to the ground, many crying out to God with screams for mercy. Word soon spread about these surprising events.

McGready and the other ministers immediately arranged another camp meeting in late July 1800 at Gasper River. The huge crowd that gathered, approximately 8,000 people, mostly in wagons, came from up to 100 miles away.

McGready described one of the evening meetings where a Presbyterian minister preached to the multitude by the flickering glow of faming torches:

> The power of God seemed to shake the whole assembly. Toward the close of the sermon, the cries of the distressed arose almost as loud as his voice. After the congregation was dismissed the solemnity increased, till the greater part of the multitude seemed engaged in the most solemn matter. No person seemed to wish to go home—hunger and sleep seemed to affect nobody—eternal things were the vast concern. Here awakening and converting work was to be found in every part of the multitude; and even some things strangely and wonderfully new to me (*Christian History* 1989, 25).

These frontier revivals became a new emphasis in American revivalism. By 1802 these outdoor gatherings, combined with camping in tents and wagons, were called "camp meetings." They spread across the frontier settlements. Meetings in the open, or in large tents, featured fiery evangelists. The sawdust trails—laid down to settle the dust or soak up the moisture on the ground—became paths where repentant sinners made their way to the front of the meetings, often with tears or loud cries of anguish.

## 1801

### *August—Cane Ridge, America (Barton Stone)*

Impressed by the revivals in 1800, Barton Stone, a Presbyterian minister, organized similar meetings in 1801 in his area at Cane Ridge, northeast of Lexington. A huge crowd of approximately 12,500 attended in more than 125 wagons, including people from Ohio and Tennessee. At that time, Lexington, the largest town in Kentucky, contained less than 1,800 citizens. Presbyterian, Methodist, and Baptist preachers and circuit riders formed preaching teams, speaking simultaneously in different parts of the campgrounds, all aiming for conversions.

James Finley, later a Methodist circuit rider, described it:

> The noise was like the roar of Niagara. The vast sea of human beings seemed to be agitated as if by a storm. I counted seven ministers, all preaching at one time, some on stumps, others in wagons and one standing on a tree which had, in falling, lodged against another. ... I stepped up on a log where I could have a better view of the surging sea of humanity. The scene that then presented itself to my mind was indescribable. At one time I saw at least *five hundred* swept down in a moment as if a battery of a thousand guns had been opened upon them, and then immediately followed shrieks and shouts that rent the very heavens (Pratney 1994, 104).

Referring to the same gathering, the Rev. Moses Hoge wrote:

> The careless fall down, cry out, tremble, and not infrequently are affected with convulsive twitchings.... Nothing that imagination can paint, can make a stronger impression upon the mind, than one of those scenes. Sinners dropping down on every hand, shrieking, groaning, crying for mercy, convulsed; professors praying, agonizing, fainting, falling down in distress for sinners or in raptures of joy! ... As to the work in general there can be no question but it is of God. The subject of it, for the most part are deeply wounded for their sins, and can give a clear and rational account of their conversion (*Christian History* 1989, 26).

Revival in the early nineteenth century not only impacted the American frontier, but also towns and especially colleges. One widespread result in America, as in England, was the formation of missionary societies to train and direct the large numbers of converts who were filled with missionary zeal.

That Second Great Awakening produced the modern missionary movement and its societies, Bible societies, promoted the abolition of slavery, and initiated many other social reforms. The Napoleonic Wars in Europe (1803-15) and the American War of 1812 with England (1812-15) dampened revival zeal, but caused many to cry out to God for help, and fresh stirrings of revival continued after that, especially with Charles G. Finney.

## 1821

### *October 10—Adams, America (Charles Finney)*

Charles Finney became well known in revivals in the nineteenth century. A keen sportsman and young lawyer, he had a mighty empowering by God's Spirit on the night of his conversion on Wednesday, October 10, 1821. That morning the Holy Spirit convicted him on his way to work, so he spent the morning praying in the woods near his small town of Adams in New York State. There he surrendered fully to God. He walked to his law office that afternoon profoundly changed, and he assisted his employer, Squire Wright, to set up a new office. That night he was filled with the Spirit. He describes that momentous night in his autobiography:

> By evening we had the books and furniture adjusted, and I made a good fire in an open fireplace, hoping to spend the evening alone. Just at dark Squire W—, seeing that everything was adjusted, told me good night and went to his home. I had accompanied him to the door, and as I closed the door and turned around my heart seemed to be liquid within me. All my feelings seemed to rise and flow out and the thought of my heart was, "I want to pour my whole soul out to God." The rising of my soul was so great that I rushed into the room back of the front office to pray.

> There was no fire and no light in this back room; nevertheless it appeared to me as if it were perfectly light. As I went in and shut the door after me, it seemed to me as if I met the Lord

Jesus Christ face to face. It seemed to me that I saw him as I would see any other man. He said nothing, but looked at me in such a manner as to break me right down at his feet. It seemed to me a reality that he stood before me, and I fell down at his feet and poured out my soul to him. I wept aloud like a child and made such confession as I could with my choked words. It seemed to me that I bathed his feet with my tears, and yet I had no distinct impression that I touched him.

I must have continued in this state for a good while, but my mind was too much absorbed with the interview to remember anything that I said. As soon as my mind became calm enough I returned to the front office and found that the fire I had made of large wood was nearly burned out. But as I turned and was about to take a seat by the fire, I received a mighty baptism of the Holy Spirit. Without any expectation of it, without ever having the thought in my mind that there was any such thing for me, without any memory of ever hearing the thing mentioned by any person in the world, the Holy Spirit descended upon me in a manner that seemed to go through me, body and soul. I could feel the impression, like a wave of electricity, going through and through me. Indeed it seemed to come in waves of liquid love, for I could not express it in any other way. It seemed like the very breath of God. I can remember distinctly that it seemed to fan me, like immense wings.

No words can express the wonderful love that was spread abroad in my heart. I wept aloud with joy and love. I literally bellowed out the unspeakable overflow of my heart. These waves came over me, and over me, and over me, one after another, until I remember crying out, "I shall die if these waves continue to pass over me." I said, "Lord, I cannot bear any more," yet I had no fear of death (Wessel 1977, 20-22).

That night a member of the church choir that Finney led called at his office and was amazed to find the former skeptic in a "state of loud weeping" and unable to talk to him for some time. That young friend left and soon returned with an elder

from the church who was usually serious and rarely laughed.
Finney observed:

> When he came in, I was very much in the state in which I was
> when the young man went out to call him. He asked me how I
> felt and I began to tell him. Instead of saying anything he fell
> into a most spasmodic laughter. It seemed as if it was impos-
> sible for him to keep from laughing from the very bottom of
> his heart (Wessel 1977, 22).

The next morning, with "the renewal of these mighty waves
of love and salvation" flowing through him, Finney witnessed
to his employer, who was strongly convicted and later made
his peace with God. Also that morning, a deacon from the
church came to see Finney about a court case due to be tried
at ten o'clock. Finney told him he would have to find another
lawyer, saying, "I have a retainer from the Lord Jesus Christ to
plead His cause and I cannot plead yours." The astonished deacon later became more serious about God and settled his case
privately.

Finney described the immediate change in his own life and
work:

> I soon sallied forth from the office to converse with those
> whom I might meet about their souls. I had the impression,
> which has never left my mind, that God wanted me to preach
> the Gospel, and that I must begin immediately....

> I spoke with many persons that day, and I believe the Spirit of
> God made lasting impressions upon every one of them. I can-
> not remember one whom I spoke with, who was not soon after
> converted....

> In the course of the day a good deal of excitement was created
> in the village because of what the Lord had done for my soul.
> Some thought one thing and some another. At evening, with-
> out any appointment having been made, I observed that the
> people were going to the place where they usually held their
> conference and prayer meetings....

I went there myself. The minister was there, and nearly all the principal people in the village. No one seemed ready to open the meeting, but the house was packed to its utmost capacity. I did not wait for anybody, but rose and began by saying that I then knew that religion was from God. I went on and told such parts of my experience as it seemed important for me to tell. ... We had a wonderful meeting that evening, and from that day we had a meeting every evening for a long time. The work spread on every side.

As I had been a leader among the young people I immediately appointed a meeting for them, which they all attended. ... They were converted one after another with great rapidity, and the work continued among them until only one of their number was left unconverted.

The work spread among all classes, and extended itself not only through the village but also out of the village in every direction (Wessel 1977, 26-31).

Finney continued for the rest of his life in evangelism and revival. During the height of the revivals he often saw the awesome holiness of God come upon people, not only in meetings, but also in the community, bringing multitudes to repentance and conversion. For example, he preached in Boston for over a year during the revival in 1858-1859, and many reports tell of people who repented as they sailed into Boston Harbor, convicted by the Holy Spirit.

Wherever he journeyed, instead of bringing a song leader, he brought someone to pray. Often Father Nash, his companion, wasn't even in the meetings but in the woods praying. Finney emphasized Hosea 10:12: "...Break up your fallow ground, for it is time to seek the Lord, till He comes and rains righteousness on you" (NKJ). He believed that if we do our part in repentance and prayer, God will do His in sending revival.

Finney founded and taught theology at Oberlin College, which pioneered coeducation and enrolled both blacks and whites. His *Lectures on Revival* were widely read and helped to fan revival fire in America and England.

## 1858

*March—New York, America (Jeremiah Lanphier)*

Various revival movements influenced society in the nineteenth century but 1858 in America and 1859 in Britain were outstanding. As is typical, it followed a low ebb of spiritual life. Concerned Christians began praying earnestly and anticipating a new move of God's Spirit.

Revival broke out at evangelistic meetings during October 1857 in Hamilton, Canada, led by the talented Phoebe Palmer, assisted by her physician husband, Walter. Phoebe, a firebrand preacher, impacted North America and England with her speaking and writing. She wrote influential books and edited *The Guide to Holiness*, the most significant magazine on holiness at that time. Her teaching on the baptism of the Holy Ghost and endowment of power spread far and wide.

The Palmers ministered widely, fanning the flames of revival and seeing thousands converted. Prayer meetings began to proliferate across North America and in Great Britain.

Jeremiah Lanphier, a city missioner, began a weekly noon prayer meeting in Fulton Street, New York, in September 1857. By October it grew into a daily prayer meeting attended by many businessmen. Anticipation of revival grew, especially with the stock market collapse that October after a year of depression, and with the threatening clouds of the looming American Civil War (1861-65).

By the beginning of 1858, that Fulton Street prayer meeting had grown so much that they were holding three simultaneous prayer meetings in the building, and other prayer groups were starting in the city. By March, newspapers carried front-page reports of over 6,000 people attending daily prayer meetings in New York and 6,000 attending them in Pittsburgh. Daily prayer meetings were held in Washington, D.C. at five different times to accommodate the crowds.

Other cities followed the pattern. Soon a common midday sign on business premises read: "Will re-open at the close of the prayer meeting."

By May, 50,000 of New York's 800,000 people were new converts. A newspaper reported that New England was profoundly changed by the revival, and in several towns no unconverted adults could be found!

A leading Methodist paper reported these features of the revival: few sermons were needed, lay people witnessed, seekers flocked to the altar, nearly all seekers were blessed, experiences remained clear, converts had holy boldness, religion became a social topic, family altars were strengthened, nightly testimony was abundant, and conversations were marked with seriousness.

The years 1858-59 saw a million Americans become converted in a population of 30 million, and at least a million Christians were renewed, with lasting results in church attendance and moral reform in society.

## 1859

### *March 14—Ulster, Ireland (James McQuilkin)*

Revival swept Great Britain also, including the Ulster revival of 1859.

During September 1857, the same month the Fulton Street meetings began, James McQuilkin commenced a weekly prayer meeting in a village schoolhouse near Kells with three other young Irishmen. This is generally seen as the start of the Ulster revival. The first conversions in answer to their prayers came in December 1857. Through 1858 innumerable prayer meetings started, and revival was a common theme of preachers.

On Monday, March 14, 1859, James McQuilkin and his praying friends organized a great prayer meeting at the Ahoghill Presbyterian Church. Such a large crowd gathered that the building was cleared in case the galleries collapsed. Outside in the chilling rain as a layman preached with great power, hundreds knelt in repentance. This was the first of many movements of mass conviction of sin.

The revival of 1859 brought 100,000 converts into the churches of Ireland. God's Spirit moved powerfully in small and large gatherings, bringing great conviction of sin, deep repentance, and lasting moral change. Prostrations were common— people lying prostrate in conviction and repentance, unable to rise for some time.

By 1860 crime was reduced; several times the judges in Ulster had no cases to try. At one time in County Antrim no crime was reported to the police and no prisoners were held in police custody.

This revival made a greater impact on Ireland than anything known since Patrick brought Christianity there. By the end of 1860 the effects of the Ulster revival were listed as thronged services, unprecedented numbers of communicants, abundant prayer meetings, increased family prayers, unmatched Scripture reading, prosperous Sunday Schools, converts remaining steadfast, increased giving, abated vice, and reduced crime.

Revival fire ignites fire. Throughout 1859 the same deep conviction and lasting conversions revived thousands of people in Wales, Scotland, and England.

Revival in Wales found expression in glorious praise including harmonies unique to the Welsh, which involved preacher and people in turn. There, too, 100,000 converts (one-tenth of the total population) were added to the church and crime was greatly reduced.

Scotland and England were similarly visited with revival. Again, prayer increased enormously, and preaching caught fire with many anointed evangelists seeing thousands converted.

Charles Haddon Spurgeon, a Baptist minister known as the prince of preachers, considered 1859 as the high-water mark although he had already been preaching in his Metropolitan

Tabernacle in London for five years with great blessing and huge crowds.

## *May 22—Natal, South Africa (Zulus)*

The wave of revival in 1857-1859 included countries around the globe. Missionaries and visitors told of thousands being converted, and others began crying out to God to send revival to their nations.

It happened in South Africa. Revival began among the Zulu and Bantu tribes before it spilled over into the Dutch Reformed Church. Tribal people gathered in large numbers on the frontier mission stations and then took revival fire, African-style, into their villages.

On Sunday night, May 22, 1859, the Spirit of God fell on a service of the Zulus in Natal so powerfully that they prayed all night. News of this service spread rapidly, and this revival among the Zulus of Natal on the east coast ignited missions and tribal churches. It produced deep conviction of sin, immediate repentance and conversions, extraordinary praying, and vigorous evangelism.

In April 1860, at a combined missions conference, more than 370 leaders of Dutch Reformed, Methodist, and Presbyterian leaders meeting at Worcester, South Africa, discussed revival. Andrew Murray, Sr., moved to tears, had to stop speaking. His son, Andrew Murray, Jr., now well known through his books, led in prayer so powerfully that many saw that as the beginning of revival in those churches.

By June, revival had so impacted the Methodist Church in Montague village, near Worcester, that they held prayer meetings every night and three mornings a week, sometimes as early as 3 a.m. The Dutch Reformed people joined together with the Methodists with great conviction of sin to seek God in repentance, worship, and intercession. Reports reached Worcester and ignited similar prayer meetings there.

As an African servant girl sang and prayed one Sunday night at Worcester, the Holy Spirit fell on the group, and a roaring sound like approaching thunder surrounded the hall, which began to shake. Instantly, everyone burst out praying! Their pastor, Andrew Murray, Sr., had been speaking in the main sanctuary. When told of this, he ran to their meeting calling for order! No one noticed. They kept crying loudly to God for forgiveness.

All week the prayer meetings continued, beginning in silence, but "as soon as several prayers had arisen the place was shaken as before and the whole company of people engaged in simultaneous petition to the throne of grace" (Orr 1975b, 58). On the following Saturday, Andrew Murray, Sr. led the prayer meeting. After preaching, he prayed and invited others to pray. Again the sound of thunder approached and everyone prayed aloud, loudly. At first Andrew Murray tried to quiet the people, but a stranger reminded him that God was at work, and he learned to accept this noisy revival praying. People were converted. The revival spread.

Fifty men from that congregation went into full-time ministry, and the revival launched Andrew Murray, Jr. into a worldwide ministry of speaking and writing.

## 1871

### *October—New York, America (D.L. Moody)*

Dwight Lyman Moody, converted in 1855, later led powerful evangelistic campaigns in America and England. Two women in his church prayed constantly that he would be filled with the Spirit, and his yearning for God continued to increase. In 1871, while visiting New York to raise funds for churches and orphanages destroyed in the Chicago fire of October that year—in which his home, church sanctuary, and the YMCA buildings were destroyed—he had a deep encounter with God. Later he wrote:

I was crying all the time God would fill me with his Spirit. Well, one day in the city of New York—oh, what a day!—I cannot describe it, I seldom refer to it; it is almost too sacred an experience to name. Paul had an experience of which he never spoke for fourteen years. I can only say that God revealed Himself to me, and I had such an experience of His love that I had to ask him to stay his hand. I went to preaching again. The sermons were not different; I did not present any new truths; and yet hundreds were converted. I would not be placed back where I was before that blessed experience for all the world—it would be as the small dust of the balance (Moody 1900, 149).

On a visit to Britain he heard Henry Varley say, "The world has yet to see what God will do with a man fully consecrated to him." D.L. Moody resolved to be that man.

Moody worked vigorously to establish the Young Men's Christian Association (YMCA) in America and England as a means of converting and discipling youth. A Baptist minister in London, the Rev. R. Boyd, went to a meeting where Moody had just spoken and observed, "When I got to the rooms of the Young Men's Christian Association, Victoria Hall, London, I found the meeting on fire. The young men were speaking with tongues, prophesying. What on earth did it mean? Only that Moody had addressed them that afternoon" (Hyatt 1997, 141).

God's Spirit powerfully impacted people through Moody's ministry, especially in conversion and in deep commitment to God. Among the thousands converted through Moody's ministry were the famous Cambridge Seven, who were students at Cambridge University and national sportsmen, including international cricketer C. T. Studd. They all eventually served the Lord in overseas missions.

# Chapter Three

# Early Twentieth Century

## 1904

### *October 31—Loughor, Wales (Evan Roberts)*

The early years of the twentieth century ushered in unprecedented revival.

Beginning with thousands of small prayer groups all over the world, the first years of the twentieth century saw revival break out in unprecedented measure. The amazing Welsh Revival of 1904-1905 became the most powerful expression of that revival, and it, in turn, impacted the world. As news of the revival spread, and as missionaries sailed from Great Britian, fervent prayer for revival increased across the world. Powerful revivals touched India, Korea, and China— and stirred revivals in South Africa and Japan, along with fresh awakenings to Africa, Latin America, and the Pacific.

From November 1904 in Wales thousands were converted in a few months—and 100,000 within a year. Five years later 80,000 remained true to God, serving Him in the churches and the community. During the revival, crime dropped dramatically, with some judges left without any cases to try. Drunkness was halved, and many taverns went bankrupt. So many miners were converted that the pit ponies hauling coal from the mines could no longer understand their clean language and stopped, confused.

Touches of revival had stirred New Quay, Cardiganshire, on the west coast of Wales where Joseph Jenkins was minister of a Methodist church from which he led teams of revived young people in conducting testimony meetings throughout the area.

The Presbyterian evangelist, Seth Joshua, arrived there in September 1904 to find remarkable moves of the Spirit in his meetings. On Sunday, September 18, he reported that he had "never seen the power of the Holy Spirit so powerfully manifested among the people as at this place just now." His meetings lasted far into the night. His diary continued:

> Monday, September 19: Revival is breaking out here in greater power...the young people receiving the greatest measure of blessing. They break out into prayer, praise, testimony and exhortation.

> Tuesday, September 20: I cannot leave the building until 12 and even 1 o'clock in the morning—I closed the service several times and yet it would break out again quite beyond control of human power.

> Wednesday, September 21: Yes, several souls...they are not drunkards or open sinners, but are members of the visible church not grafted into the true Vine...the joy is intense.

> Thursday, September 22: We held another remarkable meeting tonight. Group after group came out to the front, seeking the "full assurance of faith."

> Friday, September 23: I am of the opinion that forty conversions took place this week. I also think that those seeking assurance may be fairly counted as converts, for they had never received Jesus as personal Saviour before (Orr 1973, 3).

Seth Joshua then held meetings at Newcastle Emlyn, at which students from the Methodist Academy attended. Among them was Sidney Evans, a roommate of Evan Roberts. The students, including Evan Roberts, attended the next Joshua meetings in Blaenannerch.

There on Thursday, September 29, Seth Joshua closed the 7 a.m. meeting before breakfast, as he cried out in Welsh, "Lord...bend us."

Evan Roberts remembered, "It was the Spirit that put the emphasis for me on 'Bend us.' 'That is what you need' said the Spirit to me. And as I went out I prayed, 'O Lord, bend me.' " During the 9 a.m. meeting, Evan Roberts eventually prayed aloud after others had prayed. He knelt with his arms over the seat in front of him, bathed in perspiration as he agonized. He recalled, "I cried out, 'Bend me! Bend me! Bend us! Oh! Oh! Oh! Oh!' " (Evans 1969, 70). Soon a motto of the revival became: "Bend the church and save the world."

Evan Roberts, in his twenties, was one of God's agents in that national revival. "For ten or eleven years I have prayed for revival," he wrote to a friend. "I could sit up all night to read or talk about revivals.... It was the Spirit that moved me to think about a revival" (Orr 1973, 4).

The young miner who later became a blacksmith had attended church as a teenager on Sunday, prayer meeting Monday, youth meeting Tuesday, congregational meeting Wednesday, temperance meeting Thursday, and class meeting Friday. Saturday night was free, probably as bath night in preparation for Sunday!

He entered the Methodist Academy in mid-September 1904. Before then, he had experienced deep encounters with God and had a vision of all Wales being lifted up to Heaven. After this he regularly slept lightly until 1 a.m., woke for hours of communion with God, and then returned to sleep. He was convinced revival would touch all Wales, and eventually he led a small band all over the country praying and preaching.

Soon after the impact of the Spirit on him at Seth Joshua's meetings, he took leave to return home to challenge his friends, especially the young people. Arriving home by train at his small village of Loughor on the south coast of Wales on October 31, 1904, Evan Roberts spoke after the usual Monday night prayer meeting to 17 young people. The Holy Spirit moved on them all in that two-hour session, and they all publicly confessed Christ as their personal Savior. He then spoke every night to increasing crowds. By the weekend, the church was packed.

Evan Roberts described the response on that Sunday evening, when by midnight the congregation was overwhelmed with tears:

> Then the people came down from the gallery, and sat close to one another. "Now," said I, "we must believe that the Spirit will come; not think He will come; not hope He will come; but firmly believe that He will come." Then I read the promises of God, and pointed out how definite they were. (Remember, I am doing all under the guidance of the Holy Spirit, and praise be to Him.) After this, the Spirit said that everyone was to pray. Pray now, not confess, not sing, not give experience, but pray and believe, and wait. And this is the prayer, "Send the Spirit now, for Jesus Christ's sake."

> The people were sitting, and only closed their eyes. The prayer began with me. Then it went from seat to seat—boys and girls—young men and maidens. Some asking in silence, some aloud, some coldly, some with warmth, some formally, some in tears, some with difficulty, some adding to it, boys and girls, strong voices, then tender voices. Oh, wonderful! I never thought of such an effect. I felt the place beginning to be filled, and before the prayer had gone half way through the chapel, I could hear some brother weeping, sobbing, and saying, "Oh, dear! dear! well! well! Oh, dear! dear!" On went the prayer, the feeling becoming more intense; the place being filled more and more (with the Spirit's presence) (Duewel 1995, 190).

Invitations came for him to speak in other churches and chapels. He usually took a small team with him to pray, witness, and sing. In November 1904 the fires of revival spread through-out Wales. Newspapers began describing the crowded meet-ings. By the end of January 1905, the papers had reported 70,000 converted in three months.

The Spirit of God convicted people as Evan Roberts insisted:

1. You must put away any unconfessed sin.

2. You must put away any doubtful habit.

3. You must obey the Spirit promptly.

4. You must confess Christ publicly.

He believed that a baptism in the Spirit was the essence of revival and that the primary condition of revival is that indi-viduals should experience such a baptism in the Spirit.

As with other evangelists and ministers, Evan Roberts tra-versed the Welsh valleys, often never preaching but sitting head-in-hands, earnestly praying. In Neath he spent a week in prayer without leaving his rooms while the revival continued to pack the churches.

Churches filled. The revival spread. Meetings continued all day as well as each night, often late into the night or through un-til morning. Crowds were getting right with God and with one another in confession, repentance, and restitution of wrongs done. People prayed fervently and worshiped God with great joy. Police had so little to do they joined the crowds in the churches, sometimes forming singing groups.

The impact of the Spirit across the churches produced new levels of unity, joy, boldness, power to witness, changed lives, and a fire from God causing people to be "fervent in spirit" (Rom. 12:11).

At the height of the revival, on November 20, 1904, two brothers, Stephen and George Jeffreys, were converted in Siloh Chapel in Maesteg, their home church in the Welsh Independent (Congregational) Church. Although initially opposed to the

Pentecostalism that emerged in Wales in 1908, they became involved in 1911.

Both were powerful evangelists in Great Britain and abroad, preaching to huge crowds and seeing hundreds healed and thousands converted. They often traveled and ministered together, and they established many churches. George's campaigns included a crusade in Birmingham with 10,000 converted and powerful ministry in Europe with 14,000 converted in Switzerland in 1934-1936. He became the founder and leader of the Elim Foursquare Alliance (Elim Pentecostal Church). Stephen also pioneered many Elim churches and worked actively with the newly formed Assemblies of God of Britain and Ireland as an independent evangelist.

## 1905

### *June 30—Mukti, India (Pandita Ramabai)*

Honored with the title *Pandita* by the Sanskrit scholars of Calcutta University, Ramabai became a Christian by the turn of the century. She mastered seven languages, translated the Bible into Marathi, and published several books including *A Life of Christ*. The Indian government issued a postage stamp in her honor in 1989, recognizing her social impact on the nation.

Ramabai established a compound for child widows and orphan girls during severe famine in her area near Pune (Poona) just south of Bombay. She called it Mukti ("salvation"). By 1901 she had 2,000 girls and women, and from January 1905 she began teaching about the need for revival. Soon over 500 people, mostly women and girls, met twice daily to pray for revival.

Ramabai heard about early moves of the Spirit in northeast India and challenged her women to leave secular studies for a time to go into the villages to preach in teams. Thirty volunteered. They met daily to pray for the endowment of the Holy Spirit.

On June 29, 1905, the Spirit moved on many of the girls. The girls saw flames engulfing one of the girls, so they raced to get a bucket of water, only to discover she was not being burned.

Then on Friday, June 30, while Ramabai taught about Jesus' love for a despised woman caught in adultery from John 8, the Holy Spirit suddenly fell on them all with great power. Everyone there began to weep and pray aloud, crying out to be baptized with the Holy Spirit and fire. One 12-year-old girl, who was normally very plain in physical appearance, became radiantly beautiful and laughed constantly. Others had visions of Jesus.

Revival spread through their mission and into many surrounding areas. Regular school activities gave way to confession, repentance, and great joy with much praise and dancing. Many were baptized in the Spirit, spoke in tongues, and were filled with zeal for evangelism and social care.

During that time a missionary, Albert Norton, visited the mission. Minnie Abrams, one of the teachers there, invited him to observe a revival prayer group in the school. He later reported the following impressions of that experience:

> One week ago I visited the Mukti Mission. Miss Abrams asked me if I should like to go into a room where about twenty girls were praying. After entering, I knelt with closed eyes by a table on one side. Presently I heard someone praying near me very distinctly in English. Among the petitions were, "O Lord, open the mouth; O Lord, open the mouth; O Lord, open the heart; O Lord, open the eyes! O Lord, open the eyes! Oh, the blood of Jesus, the blood of Jesus! Oh, give complete victory! Oh, such a blessing! Oh, such glory!"
>
> I was struck with astonishment, as I knew that there was no one in the room who could speak English, beside Miss Abrams. I opened my eyes and within three feet of me, on her knees, with closed eyes and raised hands was a woman, whom I had baptised at Kedgaon in 1899, and whom my wife and I had known intimately since as a devoted Christian worker. Her mother tongue was Marathi, and she could speak a little

Hindustani. But she was unable to speak or understand English such as she was using. But when I heard her speak English idiomatically, distinctly, and fluently, I was impressed as I should have been had I seen one, whom I knew to be dead, raised to life. A few other illiterate Marathi women and girls were speaking in English and some were speaking in other languages which none at Kedagaon understood. This was not gibberish, but it closely resembled the speaking of foreign languages to which I had listened but did not understand....

Quite a number had received the ability to speak in English, a language before unknown to them. Just why God enabled those women and girls to speak in English, instead of Tamil, Bengail, Tugulu, or some other language of India, unknown to them, I cannot say. But I have an idea that it is in mercy to us poor missionaries from Europe and America who, as a class, seem to be Doubting Thomases, in regard to the gifts and workings of the Spirit, and are not receiving the power of the Holy Ghost as we ought (Frodsham 1946, 107-108).

That powerful revival spread throughout many areas of India, with both Christians and unbelievers repenting in large numbers and being filled with the Holy Spirit and the fire of God.

Revival spread to southern India where Amy Carmichael at Dohnavur among the Tamils had been praying and longing for a visitation of the Spirit of God. In October 1905, the Spirit moved upon the people so powerfully they could neither preach nor pray aloud. They broke down weeping. Amy Carmichael wrote:

It was so startling and so awful.

...Soon the whole upper half of the church was on its face on the floor crying to God, each boy and girl, man and woman, oblivious of all others. The sound was like the sound of waves of strong wind in the trees. No separate voice could be heard. ...I had never heard of such a thing as this among Tamil people. Up in the north, of course, one knew that it had happened, but our Tamils are so stolid, so unemotional I had never imagined such a thing as this occurring" (Duewel 1995, 230).

Earlier that year, before the Mukti revival began, a revival spark had stirred in Assam, in northeast India, but it took much longer to ignite and did not spread with the intensity of the western fires. From the beginning of 1905, the Khasi hill-tribe Christians met every night to pray for revival for over 18 months. Their Welsh Presbyterian missionaries had brought news of revival in Wales that stirred them to earnest prayer. Those nightly meetings often went past 10 p.m.

One Sunday, March 4, 1906, the Bible teaching concerning the baptism of the Spirit stirred the people deeply. The Christians felt an unusual sense of the Spirit's Presence, which produced prolonged prayer, weeping, and praise. Gradually revival spread through the presbytery with powerful messages from Khasi preachers and widespread repentance.

The Baptists also reported remarkable awakenings along the wide Brahmaputra River valley. Revival spread through 1907 into all the churches of the Brahmaputra, then south into the Naga hills and then on to the Mizo tribe further south. A pagan anti-revival movement flared in 1911-12, but when a plague of rats invaded the area and demolished their food, the people suffered terribly. Refugees poured down into the plains where Christians shared their food and cared for them. So the pagan revival died out and then in 1913 and again in 1919 greater revivals of Christianity ignited the hills of northeast India.

## 1906

### *April 14—Azusa Street, Los Angeles (William Seymour)*

Early in 1906, William J. Seymour, a black Holiness pastor, studied briefly at Charles Parham's short-term Bible School in Houston, Texas. Segregation laws in that state prohibited blacks from joining the classes, so he sat in the hall and listened through the doorway.

Parham previously had conducted classes at a Bible College in Topeka, Kansas, where on January 1, 1901, a lady named Agnes Ozman spoke in tongues when Parham laid hands on her and prayed for her to be baptized in the Spirit. Soon Parham and half of the 34 students also spoke in tongues. They taught that the gift of tongues was the initial evidence of baptism in the Holy Spirit. (In the early days they believed that these tongues were gifts of other languages to be used in missionary evangelism!) Those events have been seen as the beginning of Pentecostalism in America.

A small holiness church in Los Angeles invited William Seymour to preach with the possibility of becoming pastor of the church. His first sermon there, from Acts 2:4, emphasized being filled with the Spirit and speaking in tongues. When he arrived for his second service, he found himself locked out of the building!

Seymour then began cottage meetings in a home on Bonnie Brae Street, which still exists as a Pentecostal landmark. Many there, including Seymour, began speaking in tongues, and the numbers in attendance grew until the weight of the crowd broke the front verandah, so they had to move. They found an old, two-story, weatherboard stable and warehouse at 312 Azusa Street, which had previously been an African Episcopal Methodist church.

So Seymour, now leader of The Apostolic Faith Mission, began meetings there on Easter Saturday, April 14, 1906. About 100 attended, including both blacks and whites. The Spirit of God moved powerfully on that little mission. Many were baptized in the Spirit with speaking in tongues and prophecies. Four days later on Wednesday, April 18, the day of the San Francisco earthquake, the *Los Angeles Times* began carrying articles about the weird babble of tongues and wild scenes at Azusa Street.

Not only was the racial mixture unusual, but also the newspaper reports—usually critical of those noisy Pentecostal meetings—drew both Christians and unbelievers, poor and rich, to investigate. Soon crowds crammed into the building to investigate or mock. Hundreds were saved, baptized in the Spirit, and ignited for apostolic-style mission, which includes prayers for healing and outreach in evangelism and overseas mission.

The exploding Pentecostal movement around the world usually traces its origins to Azusa Street, from where fire spread across the globe. For example, John G. Lake had visited the mission at Azusa Street. In 1908 he pioneered Pentecostal missions in South Africa where, after five years, he had established 500 black and 125 white congregations. Later he established healing rooms where thousands were healed through medicine and prayer at Spokane, Washington, which became known as the healthiest city in America at that time.

The Azusa Street revival touched the world, although it was not the first time a church experienced the gifts of the Spirit in revival. For example, Edward Irving, a Scottish Presbyterian pastor in London, began teaching on charismata in England and Scotland in 1825. By early 1830 parishioners near Glasgow experienced tongues and prophecies, and by 1831 these were common in his London church. Expelled by the London Presbytery from his church in 1832 because of his views on Christology and because he gave permission for unordained men and women to give prophecies, he formed a church of 800, which became the Catholic Apostolic Church. His followers were nicknamed Irvingites. Irving died in 1834, and the church he founded gradually adopted liturgical elements but lasted barely another 40 years.

In contrast, on August 19, 1886, the Church of God (Cleveland), one of the oldest and largest Pentecostal bodies, was instituted as a small group called the Christian Union in Monroe County, Tennessee, to "sit together as the Church of God to transact business as the same." In 1892 they formed a second fellowship 12 miles away in Cherokee County, in the mountains of North Carolina, where in 1896 at the Shearer Schoolhouse 130 believers experienced gifts of the Spirit including tongues and healings in their noisy meetings. Their churches grew and multiplied in spite of violent persecution for a decade with churches and homes burned, and people flogged, shot at, and stoned. Their headquarters became established in Cleveland, Tennessee, where on January 11, 1907, they adopted the name, Church of God. From 1906, hearing of similar developments at Azusa Street, they taught the baptism of the Holy Spirit and gifts of the Spirit much more boldly.

So, to briefly summarize what we've already covered, the Great Awakening of the eighteenth century produced many revived churches and brought the Methodist Church into being. The evangelical revival produced movements, including the holiness churches of the nineteenth century. Those movements prepared the way for the surprising development of the Pentecostal churches and then the charismatic movement of the twentieth century.

## 1907

### *January 7—Pyongyang, Korea*

In 1907, Presbyterian missionaries, hearing of revival in Wales and of similar revival among Welsh Presbyterian work in Assam, prayed earnestly for the same in Korea. Beginning on January 2, 1907, church representatives gathered for ten days at the annual New Year Bible study course at Pyongyang, then the capital of Korea. A spirit of prayer broke out. The meetings carried on day after day, with confessions of sins, weeping, and trembling.

Then on Monday night, January 7, so many wanted to pray that the leaders called all 1,500 of them to pray aloud together. Their prayers mingled with public confession, much weeping, and many dropping prostrate on the floor in agonies of repentance.

It astounded observers. The delegates of the New Year gathering later returned to their churches, taking with them this spirit of prayer, which strongly impacted the churches of the nation with revival. That pattern of simultaneous prayer became a feature of Korean church life. Everywhere, conviction of sin, confession, and restitution were common. Within two months, 2,000 people were converted, and by the middle of 1907, 30,000 had become Christians.

Persecution at the hands of the Japanese and then the Russian and Chinese communists killed thousands of Christians, but still the church grew in fervent prayer. Prior to the Russian invasion, thousands of North Koreans gathered every morning at 5 a.m. Sometimes 10,000 people were gathered in one place for prayer each morning.

Throughout Korea, daily early morning prayer meetings became common, as did nights of prayer. Even today, more than a million gather every morning around 5 a.m. for prayer in the churches. Prayer and fasting is normal. Churches have over 100 prayer retreats in the hills, called "prayer mountains," to which thousands go to pray, often with fasting. Healings and supernatural manifestations continue. Koreans have sent over 10,000 missionaries into other Asian countries, and Korea now has the largest Presbyterian and Methodist churches in the world.

David Yonggi Cho has seen amazing growth in Seoul, where he is senior pastor of a Full Gospel church of 800,000, with more than 25,000 home cell groups and sustained church growth. During the week, over 3,000 people a day and over 5,000 on weekends pray at their prayer mountain.

## 1909

### *July 4—Valparaiso, Chile (Willis Hoover)*

Minnie Abrams, who worked at the Mukti Mission in India during the 1905 revival there, sent an account of it in 1907 to her friends, Willis and Mary Hoover, Methodist missionaries in Chile. They began praying with their congregation for a similar revival in Chile. From February, up to 200 prayed all night every Saturday. Many confessed sins openly and made restitution for wrongs done. That prepared the way for the revival that burst on them on Sunday, July 4, 1909. Willis Hoover wrote:

> Saturday night was an all night of prayer, during which four vain young ladies (three of them were in the choir) fell to the floor under the power of the Spirit. One of them, after lying a long time, arose and with remarkable power began to exhort saying, "The Lord is coming soon and commands us to get ready." The effect produced was indescribable.

> The following morning in Sunday School, at ten o'clock, a daze seemed to rest upon the people. Some were unable to rise after the opening prayer which had been like "the sound of many waters," and all were filled with wonder. ... From that time on the atmosphere seemed charged by the Holy Spirit, and people fell on the floor, or broke out speaking in other tongues, or singing in the Spirit, in a way impossible in their natural condition. On one occasion a woman, a young lady, and a girl of twelve were lying on the floor in different parts of the prayer room, with eyes closed and silent. Suddenly, as with one voice, they burst forth into a song in a familiar tune but in unknown tongues, all speaking the same words. After a verse or two they became silent; then again suddenly, another tune, a verse or two, and silence. This was repeated until they had sung ten tunes, always using the same words and keeping in perfect time together as if led by some invisible chorister (Frodsham 1946, 177-178).

Within two months the congregation grew from 300 to 1,000 and the revival spread to other cities. Hostile press publicity and accusations caused Willis Hoover to leave the Methodist denomination, but he established the Pentecostal Methodist Church, which now has over 600,000 members in Chile.

## 1921

### *March 7—Lowestoft, England (Douglas Brown)*

Douglas Brown, a Baptist minister in South London, had conversions in his church every Sunday. In obedience to God, he began itinerant evangelism in 1921, and within 18 months he addressed over 1,700 meetings and saw revival in his evangelistic ministry.

The Lord had convicted him about leaving his pastorate for mission work. Although reluctant to leave his church, he finally surrendered. He described it this way:

> God laid hold of me in the midst of a Sunday evening service, and he nearly broke my heart while I was preaching. I went back to my vestry and locked the door, and threw myself down on the hearthrug in front of the vestry fireplace brokenhearted. Why? I do not know. My church was filled. I loved my people, and I believe my people loved me. I do not say they ought to, but they did. I was as happy there as I could be. I had never known a Sunday there for fifteen years without conversions. That night I went home and went straight up to my study. ... I had no supper that night. Christ laid his hand on a proud minister, and told him that he had not gone far enough, that there were reservations in his surrender, and he wanted him to do a piece of work that he had been trying to evade. I knew what he meant. All November that struggle went on, but I would not give way; I knew God was right, and I knew I was wrong. I knew what it would mean for me, and I was not prepared to pay the price. ... All through January God wrestled with me. There is a love that will not let us go. Glory be to God! ...

> It was in February 1921, after four months of struggle that there came the crisis. Oh, how patient God is! On the Saturday night I wrote out my resignation to my church, and it was marked with my own tears. I loved the church, but I felt that if I could not be holy I would be honest; I felt that I could not go on preaching while I had a contention with God. That night

the resignation lay on my blotter, and I went to bed but not to sleep. As I went out of my bedroom door in the early hours of the morning I stumbled over my dog. If ever I thanked God for my dog I did that night. As I knelt at my study table, the dog licked his master's face; he thought I was ill; when Mike was doing that I felt I did not deserve anybody to love me; I felt an outcast.

Then something happened. I found myself in the loving embrace of Christ for ever and ever; and all power and joy and blessedness rolled in like a deluge. How did it come? I cannot tell you. Perhaps I may when I get to heaven. All explanations are there, but the experience is here. That was two o'clock in the morning. God had waited four months for a man like me; and I said, "Lord Jesus, I know what you want; you want me to go into mission work. I love Thee more than I dislike that." I did not hear any rustling of angels' wings. I did not see any sudden light (Griffin 1992, 17-18).

Hugh Ferguson, the Baptist minister at London Road Baptist Church in Lowestoft on the East Anglia coast, had invited Douglas Brown to preach at a mission there from Monday to Friday, March 7-11. The missioner arrived by train, ill. However, he spoke on Monday night and at meetings on Tuesday morning, afternoon, and night. The power of the Holy Spirit moved among the people from the beginning. On Wednesday night "inquirers" packed the adjacent schoolroom for counseling and prayer. Sixty to seventy young people were converted that night, along with older people. Each night more people packed the "inquiry room" after the service. So the mission was extended indefinitely. Douglas Brown returned to his church for the weekend and continued with the mission the next Monday. By the end of March the meetings were moved from the 700-seat Baptist Church to the 1100-seat capacity of St. John's Anglican Church.

Revival had begun. Although Douglas Brown was the main speaker in many places, ministers of most denominations found they, too, were evangelizing. Revival meetings multiplied in the fishing center of Yarmouth as well in Ipswich, Norwich, Cambridge, and elsewhere. Scottish fishermen working out of Yarmouth in the winter were strongly impacted and took revival fire to Scottish fishing towns and villages in the summer. Jock Troup, a Scottish evangelist, visited East Anglia during the revival and then ministered powerfully in Scotland.

At the same time, the Spirit of God moved strongly in Ireland, especially in Ulster in 1921 through the work of W.P. (William Patteson) Nicholson, a fiery Irish evangelist. This was at the time when Northern Ireland received parliamentary autonomy accompanied by tension and bloodshed. Edwin Orr was converted then, although not through W.P. Nicholson. Orr reported that:

> Nicholson's missions were the evangelistic focus of the movement: 12,409 people were counselled in the inquiry rooms; many churches gained additions, some a hundred, some double; …prayer meetings, Bible classes and missionary meetings all increased in strength. … Ministerial candidates doubled (Griffin 1992, 87).

## 1936

### June 24—Gahini, Rwanda (East African Revival)

Africa has seen many powerful revivals, such as the Belgian Congo outpouring with C.T. Studd in 1914. "The whole place was charged as if with an electric current. Men were falling, jumping, laughing, crying, singing, confessing and some shaking terribly," he reported. "As I led in prayer the Spirit came down in mighty power sweeping the congregation. My whole body trembled with the power. We saw a marvellous sight, people literally filled and drunk with the Spirit" (World Evangelism Crusade 1954, 12-15).

Accounts like that are typical of the continuing moves of God's Spirit in Africa. Early this century an estimated 10 percent of the population was Christian. The Christian population has reached 45-50 percent of Africa south of the Sahara. The number of African Christians is estimated to be 400 million, half the population. Much of that growth came through widespread revivals such as the East African revival in 1936 and the incredible mushrooming of independent churches.

Evangelical Anglican missionaries of the Church Missionary Society, working in the east-central African countries of Rwanda, Burundi, and Uganda, emphasized the Keswick teaching of new birth, being filled with the Holy Spirit, and living in victory. This teaching undergirded the East African revival, which continued for 50 years after its beginning in the 1930's.

The Rwanda mission, founded in 1920, experienced local revivals in the late 1920's and early 1930's. Increasingly, people prayed. By 1936, thousands were praying. Then powerful revival broke out at the mission station at Ghini in Rwanda on Wednesday, June 24, 1936.

> It seemed as though the Holy Spirit with His unseen hand gathered together the hospital staff, men from the nearby village, and others in a room with the hospital. They prayed and sang, and some were smitten down under a tremendous conviction of sin. Revival swept into the girl's school, and similar manifestations came from five different centers across the mission. Everywhere the mysterious power of the Holy Spirit was at work (Duewel 1995, 300).

The revival spread to the theological college where 50 students caught the fire. During the mid-year holiday period, 70 evangelists traveled in revival teams of two or three into the villages. The African Rwanda Mission had 20,000 converts by 1942 in 700 village congregations with 1,400 trained workers, including five ordained priests.

The famous East African revival, which began in Rwanda in June 1936, rapidly spread to the adjacent countries of Burundi, Uganda, and the Congo, then further around. The Holy Spirit moved upon mission schools and spread to churches and whole communities, producing deep repentance and changed lives. Anglican Archdeacon Arthur Pitt-Pitts wrote in September 1936:

> I have been to all the stations where this Revival is going on, and they all have the same story to tell. The fire was alight in all of them before the middle of June, but during the last week in June, it burst into a wild flame which, like the African grass fire before the wind, cannot be put out (Osborn 1991, 21).

That East African revival continued for 40 to 50 years and helped to establish a new zeal for enthusiastic holiness in African Christianity. It confronted demonic strongholds and began to prepare churches to cope with the horrors of massacres and warfare of later years.

# Chapter Four

# Mid-Twentieth Century

**1947**

*April-July—North America (Healing Evangelism Revival)*

Following World War II, especially in 1947-48, the Lord began imparting powerful ministries to people who later had worldwide impact. These included William Branham, Kathryn Kuhlman, Oral Roberts, Billy Graham, and T.L. and Daisy Osborn.

William Branham reported that on Tuesday, May 7, 1946, an angel spoke to him saying:

> Fear not, I am sent from the presence of Almighty God to tell you that your peculiar life and your misunderstood ways have been to indicate that God has sent you to take a gift of divine healing to the people of the world. *If you will be sincere, and can get the people to believe you, nothing shall stand before your prayer, not even cancer* (Riss 1988, 106).

He became renowned for accurate words of knowledge and amazing healings in his powerful evangelism.

On Sunday, April 27, 1947, when Kathryn Kuhlman began a teaching series on the Holy Spirit in Franklin, Pennsylvania, a woman in the audience was healed of a tumor and testified about it the following night. That marked the beginning of

Kathryn Kuhlman's 30 years of incredible healing evangelism. Based at Pittsburgh, Pennsylvania, starting in 1948, she held regular services in Carnegie Hall and the First Presbyterian Church, developed a daily radio ministry, and produced over 500 telecasts for the CBS network. For ten years she regularly filled the 7,000-seat Shrine Auditorium in Los Angeles at her monthly miracle services there.

On May 14, 1947, following seven months of intensive prayer, including fasting, Oral Roberts received direction from God about beginning his now-famous healing evangelistic ministry. He himself had been healed through prayer at age 17 after being bedridden with tuberculosis for five months. In 1948 he used a tent that seated 2,000 people, and by 1953 he needed a tent that seated 12,500. By 1956 his monthly magazine, *Abundant Life*, had a circulation of over a million. In 1965 he opened a college, which later became Oral Roberts University, now with 4,500 students. By the 1980's 15 million copies of his books had been sold, and thousands of people continue the healing and evangelistic ministry he began.

On June 24, 1947, Henrietta Mears, Christian Education Director at First Presbyterian Church of Hollywood, spoke at a teachers and leaders conference at Forest Home in the nearby mountains. A group of young leaders, including the newly converted Bill Bright (later founder of Campus Crusade for Christ), met late that night for prayer with Henrietta Mears, confessing sin with much weeping and crying out to God.

God moved upon them, giving a mighty vision of college campuses teeming with students needing to be saved. Students were the key to leadership for revival around the world.

Annual College Briefing Conferences were then held at Forest Home. Billy Graham and Edwin Orr spoke at the 1949 conference there, where Billy Graham also experienced a deep infilling of the Holy Spirit as the Presence of God engulfed him while he prayed alone on a mountain. His Los Angeles crusade later that year attracted wide press coverage and launched him into an international ministry.

In July 1947 Tommy and Daisy Osborn, Pentecostal pastors in Oregon, were deeply moved at a camp meeting by a message about seeing Jesus. They had returned to America after an unsuccessful time as missionaries in India in 1945-6 where sickness plagued them. Following that camp meeting T.L. Osborn wrote:

> The next morning at six o'clock, I was awakened by a vision of Jesus Christ as he came into our room. I looked upon him. I saw Him like I see anyone. No tongue can tell of His splendour and beauty. No language can express the magnificence and power of His person.

> I lay there as one that was dead, unable to move a finger or toe, awe-stricken by His presence. Water poured from my eyes, though I was not conscious of weeping, so mighty was His presence.

> Of all I had heard and read about Him, the half had never been told me. His hands were beautiful; they seemed to vibrate with creative ability. His eyes were as streams of love, pouring forth into my innermost being. His feet, standing amidst clouds of transparent glory, seemed to be as pillars of justice and integrity. His robes were white as the light. His presence, enhanced with love and power, drew me to Him.

> After perhaps thirty minutes of utter helplessness, I was able to get out of bed to the floor, where I crawled into my little study and lay on my face on the floor in full surrender of my entire life to Him whom I had come to know as LORD.

> I lay there on my face until the afternoon. When I came out of that room, I was a new man. Jesus had become the Master of my life. I knew the truth; *He is alive; He is more than a dead religion.*

> My life was changed. I would never be the same. Old traditional values began to fade away, and I felt impressed daily by

a new and increasing sense of reverence and serenity. Everything was different. I wanted to please *Him. That is all that mattered since that unforgettable morning* (Osborn 1986, 394-5).

In September 1947 the Osborns attended a meeting where William Branham healed the sick and cast out demons, including deliverance of a deaf-mute girl who then heard and spoke perfectly. T.L. Osborn reported:

> When I witnessed that and many other miracles, there seemed to be a thousand voices whirling over my head, saying over and over, "*You can do that! That's the Bible way! Peter and Paul did it that way! That's the way Jesus did it. That proves that the Bible way works today! You can do that! That's what God wants you to do!*"

> We went home in total awe and reverent exuberance. We had witnessed the Bible in action. It was the thing I had always longed for. At last, I had seen God do what He promised to do through a human person. Our entire lives were changed that very night (Osborn 1986, 397).

Since then the Osborns have ministered to millions, preached to crowds of 20,000 to 250,000 in crusades in 76 countries, and led hundreds of thousands of people to Jesus Christ. Vast numbers have been healed, including the deaf, blind, and crippled. Body organs have been recreated and restored, cancers have died and vanished, lepers have been healed, and the dead have been raised.

Most of their powerful evangelism and healing ministry have been with huge crowds in developing nations. They regularly established 400 churches a year in these nations.

## 1948

### *February 12—Saskatchewan, Canada (Sharon Bible School)*

A revival movement that came to be called the Latter Rain revival (from Joel 2:28) began suddenly in the Sharon Orphanage and Schools, including the Bible School, in North

Battleford, Saskatchewan, Canada. Teachers from the Bible School had been deeply impressed by the words of knowledge and healings at meetings conducted by William Branham in 1947 in Vancouver. They and the students began praying and fasting and studying the Scriptures with new intensity from November 1947.

On Thursday, February 12, 1948, the staff and most of the 70 students had gathered in the largest classroom for devotion when the Holy Spirit fell on their gathering. Ern Hawtin, a teacher there, described it in their magazine, the *Sharon Star*:

> Some students were under the power of God on the floor, others were kneeling in adoration and worship before the Lord. The anointing deepened until the awe was upon everyone. The Lord spoke to one of the brethren, "Go and lay hands upon a certain student and pray for him." While he was in doubt and contemplation one of the sisters who had been under the power of God went to the brother saying the same words, and naming the identical student he was to pray for. He went in obedience and a revelation was given concerning the student's life and future ministry. After this a long prophecy was given with minute details concerning the great thing God was about to do. The pattern for the revival and many details concerning it were given (Hyatt 1997, 187-8).

They spent Friday studying the Scriptures for insight into these events. Ern Hawtin reported that the next day, Saturday, February 14:

> It seemed that all heaven broke loose upon our souls, and heaven came down to greet us. Soon a visible manifestation of gifts was received when candidates were prayed over, and many as a result were healed, as gifts of healing were received (Hyatt 1997, 188).

He continued, "Day after day the Glory and power of God came among us. Great repentance, humbling, fasting and prayer prevailed in everyone" (Riss 1988, 112-113).

Through the publications, camp meetings, conventions, and visits of pastors and teachers from Sharon to churches and meetings across Canada and America, thousands were touched by God in this fresh outpouring of His Spirit. Stanley Frodsham, then editor of the Assemblies of God magazine, *Pentecostal Evangel*, visited churches touched by this revival and gave it strong support.

Yet, many Pentecostal denominations rejected this move that emphasized laying on of hands for the impartation of spiritual gifts, the recognition of apostles and prophets in the church, and the gift of prophecy for directing and commissioning ministerial candidates and for church government. However, the Latter Rain revival, along with the healing revivals during the 1950's, had a strong influence on the charismatic renewal of the 1960's and 1970's.

## 1949

### *Hebrides Islands, Scotland (Duncan Campbell)*

Following the trauma of World War II, spiritual life was at a low ebb in the Scottish Hebrides. In 1949, from their cottage near Barvas village on the Isle of Lewis (the largest of the Hebrides Islands in the bleak northwest of Scotland), Peggy and Christine Smith, aged 84 and 82, started praying constantly for revival. God showed Peggy in a dream that revival was coming. Months later, early one winter's morning as the sisters were praying, God give them an unshakable conviction that revival was near.

Peggy asked her minister, James Murray Mackay, to call the church leaders to prayer. Three nights a week, for several months, the leaders prayed together. One night, having begun to pray at 10 p.m., a young deacon from the Free Church read Psalm 24 and challenged everyone to be clean before God. As they waited on God, His awesome Presence swept over them in the barn at 4 a.m.

Mackay invited a man named Duncan Campbell to come and lead meetings. Within two weeks he came, despite having previous engagements. God had intervened and changed Duncan's plans and commitments. At the close of his first meeting in the Presbyterian church in Barvas, the travel-weary preacher received the invitation to join an all-night prayer meeting! Thirty people gathered for prayer in a nearby cottage. Duncan Campbell described it:

> God was beginning to move, the heavens were opening, we were there on our faces before God. Three o'clock in the morning came, and God swept in. About a dozen men and women lay prostrate on the floor, speechless. Something had happened; we knew that the forces of darkness were going to be driven back, and men were going to be delivered. We left the cottage at 3 am to discover men and women seeking God. I walked along a country road, and found three men on their faces, crying to God for mercy. There was a light in every home, no one seemed to think of sleep (Whittaker 1984, 159).

When Duncan Campbell and his friends arrived at the church that morning, it was already crowded. People had gathered from all over the island, some coming in buses and vans. No one discovered who told them to come. God led them. Large numbers were converted as God's Spirit convicted multitudes of sin, many lying prostrate, many weeping. At the end of that amazing day in the church, Duncan Campbell pronounced the benediction; but then a young man began to pray aloud. He prayed for 45 minutes. Once more the church filled with people repenting, and the service continued until 4 a.m. the next morning before Duncan could pronounce the benediction again.

> Even then he was unable to go home to bed. As he was leaving the church a messenger told him, "Mr. Campbell, people are gathered at the police station, from the other end of the parish; they are in great spiritual distress. Can anyone here come along and pray with them?"

Campbell went and what a sight met him. Under the still starlit sky he found men and women on the road, others by the side of a cottage, and some behind a peat stack—all crying to God for mercy. The revival had come (Whittaker 1984, 160).

His mission continued for five weeks. Services were held from early morning until late at night and into the early hours of the morning. The revival spread to the parishes around Barvas with similar scenes of repentance, prayer, and preaching. People sensed the awesome Presence of God everywhere. That move of God, which came in answer to prevailing prayer, continued in that area into the 1950's and peaked again on the previously resistant island of North Uist in 1957. Meetings were again crowded, and night after night people cried out to God for salvation.

## 1951

### *June 4—City Bell, Argentina (Ed Miller)*

Edward Miller, a Pentecostal missionary, saw revival break out in Argentina. God had told him to call his small church to pray every night from 8 p.m. to midnight beginning on a Monday. Their little group prayed for three nights, mostly silently except for their missionary, Ed Miller. No one seemed to have any leading, except one lady felt she was told to hit the table, but she wouldn't do anything so strange.

On the fourth night, Ed Miller led the group in singing around the table, and hit it as they sang. Eventually others did the same. Then the lady did. Immediately the Spirit of God fell. They were baptized powerfully in the Spirit. They heard the sound of strong wind. Their little church filled. People were convicted, weeping, and praying.

By Saturday, teams were going out in powerful evangelism. Two teenage girls were weeping in the street; two doctors mocked them, but listened to their testimonies and were convicted. They knelt there in the street and asked for prayer.

Two church members visited a lady whose mother was paralyzed in bed for five years. They prayed for her, and she got up and drank tea with them. Two elderly people visited a man in a coma. When they prayed for a cripple with a liver damaged from drink, he was healed.

A young man, Alexander, and his band of rebels sat in the front row of a revival meeting, aiming to disrupt it. God convicted him and he repented. His gang began to leave but fell under the power of the Spirit on the way out. All were converted. Two of them later went to the Bible School.

Ed Miller taught at the Bible Training Institute in 1951 in the little town of City Bell, near Buenos Aires. In June he was led to cancel lectures so the whole Bible School could pray every day. He announced this on the first Sunday in June.

That night Alexander, the former rebel leader, a teenager of Polish descent, was praying long after midnight out in the fields when he sensed something pressing down on him, an intense light surrounding him, and a heavenly being enfolding him. Terrified, he ran back to the Institute.

> The heavenly visitor entered the Institute with him, and in a few moments all the students were awake with the fear of God upon them. They began to cry out in repentance as God by his Spirit dealt with them. The next day the Spirit of God came again upon Alexander as he was given prophecies of God's moving in far off countries. The following day Alexander again saw the Lord in the Spirit, but this time he began to speak slowly and distinctly the words he heard from the angel of God. No one could understand what he was saying, however, until another lad named Celsio (with even less education than Alexander), overcome with the Spirit of God markedly upon him, began to interpret.... These communications (written because he choked up when he tried to talk) were a challenge from God to pray and indeed the Institute became a centre of prayer till the vacation time, when teams went out to

preach the kingdom. It was the beginning of new stirrings of the Spirit across the land (Pytches 1989, 49-51).

The Bible Institute continued in prayer for four months from that initial outpouring of the glory of God on Monday, June 4. They prayed eight to ten hours a day, with constant weeping. Bricks became saturated with their tears. Weeping, one student prayed against a plaster wall daily. After six hours his tear stains reached the floor. After eight hours his tears began to form a puddle on floor.

Two students went to a nearby town, where they wept and prayed for three to four weeks. Then the Holy Spirit led them to hold tent meetings drawing crowds that filled the tent. The Lord moved on the crowds powerfully. Students gave prophecies at the Bible School about God filling the largest auditoriums and stadiums in Argentina and in other countries.

In 1952 Edwin Orr visited each of the 25 states and territories in neighboring Brazil, seeing powerful moves of the Spirit in his meetings, which were supported by all denominations. The evangelical church council declared that the year of 1952 saw the first of such a general spiritual awakening in the country's history. Many meetings had to be moved into soccer stadiums, some churches increased in numbers by 50 percent in one week, and the revival movement continued in local churches in Brazil.

Also in 1952 Tommy Hicks was conducting a series of meetings in California when God showed him a vision. While he was praying, he saw a map of South America covered with a vast field of golden wheat ripe for harvesting. The wheat turned into human beings calling him to come and help them.

He wrote a prophecy in his Bible about going by air to that land before two summers would pass. Three months later, after an evangelistic crusade, a pastor's wife in California gave that same prophecy to him. He was invited to Argentina in 1954 and had enough money to buy a one-way air ticket to Buenos Aires.

On his way there after meetings in Chile, the word *Peron* came to his mind. He asked the airline stewardess if she knew what it meant. She told him that Peron was the President of Argentina. After he made an appointment with the Minister of Religion, wanting to see the President, he prayed for the Minister's secretary who was limping, and he was healed. So the Minister made an appointment for Hicks to see the President. Through prayer, the President was healed of an ugly eczema, and gave Hicks the use of a stadium and free access to the state radio and press.

The revival campaign shifted into Argentina's largest arena, the Hurricane Football Stadium, seating 110,000, which overflowed. During nightly meetings over two months, 300,000 people registered decisions for Christ, and many were healed at every meeting.

## 1962

### *August 15—Santo, Vanuatu (Paul Grant)*

Australian missionary pastor-teacher, Paul Grant, saw early stirrings of revival in Vanuatu. He commented in an unpublished report:

It is important to note the following components in the lead-up to later visitation and reviving:

1. A shared concern of missionaries for revival.

2. A significantly developed interest in the quickening power of the Spirit among west Ambai church members and leaders through teaching of the Scriptures and news of revival and the power-works of the Spirit in other parts of the world, e.g. a Series of talks on the East Africa revival, the Welsh revival, signs and wonders and healings as reported from the Apostolic Church in Papua New Guinea, and inspiring records in other magazines.

3. An emphasis on prayer meetings, both between missionaries and in local churches.

4. Regular and frequent prayers for a visitation of God's Spirit by Apostolic Churches around the world. The first Monday night of each month was observed as a prayer night for world-wide missions.

5. Concentrated, sustained Scripture teaching in the class-rooms of the primary school where students later would experience the power of God.

By 1961 I had spent nine years among the people learning many valuable lessons in cross-cultural service and feeling myself being incorporated into their "family" stage by stage. Church services were free and open for much congregational participation. During 1961 in the construction and opening of a new school building a spirit of prayer was noticeably intense.

A week of prayer prior to the special ceremonies for the dedication of the school building was a markedly powerful time. On Santo Island in the town of Luganville a non-professional missionary of the Apostolic Church, a builder, was experiencing a surge of power in the local church fellowship consisting principally of people from Ambae working in this urban situation. Then came a series of significant episodes.

Beginning in the Santo church on Sunday, August 15th, 1962, and continuing there and in churches on Ambae (commencing in Tafala village in October) over a period of about 12 weeks the power of God moved upon young people. There were many instances of glossolalia, healings, prophetic utterances, excitation, loud acclamations to God in public services, incidents of deep conviction of sin, conversions, restitutions, and other manifestations of holiness of life.

From diary and report records I have the following observations:

1. Shouts and liberty and outstretched arms, fervent praying by all...for one hour (24 August).

2. I've never seen such passionate fervency (7 September).

3. Abraham (young man) through the day had sought the Lord...at night he was filled with the Spirit (8 October).

4. ...these baptisms (in the Spirit) have produced a reverence and spiritual quickening of depth and sincerity (14 October).

5. ...reverence is prominent.

6. ...Stanley (young man) in the classroom broke forth in other tongues during a Bible lesson on 2 Corinthians 4 ...prayer...four students committed themselves to Christ (2 December).

7. Thomas (an older man) told me he was drawn by the Spirit to the school building to listen (3 December).

8. Williamson...has thrown away his cigarettes...agitated over temptation...asked for prayer (3 December).

9. ...infusion of new life and power in the weekly meetings (2 January 1963).

This visitation resulted in a liveliness not known before. Initially it was mainly among young people. In later months and years it spread among all age groups and to my present knowledge was the first such visitation in the history of the Christian Church in Vanuatu. To me, the gratification I gained centred upon the following particulars:

1. The Holy Spirit had animated and empowered a people who were well taught in the Scriptures. Records show a lift in spiritual vitality in all the village churches.

2. It brought the church as a whole into a more expressive, dynamic dimension and also a charismatic gift function. They were much more able to gain victory over spirit forces so familiar to them.

3. It began to hasten the maturation processes in developing leadership.

4. The reality matched the doctrinal stand of the church. There was now no longer a disparity.

5. It confirmed to me the very great importance of being "steadfast, unmovable, always abounding in the work of the Lord forasmuch as you know that your labour is not in vain in the Lord" (1 Corinthians 15:58).

6. It led to significant outreach in evangelism, both personal and group....

In the following years some of the young men and women served God in evangelistic teams, school teaching, urban witness, government appointments, and as pastors and elders to their own people. One of them has with his wife been an effective missionary...in Papua New Guinea (Grant 1986, 7-10).

More recently, fresh impacts of the Spirit have stirred Vanuatu. For example, in a personal letter from Ruth Rongo, of Tongoa Island, dated August 28, 1991, she says:

I've just come back from an evangelism ministry. It lasted for three months. God has done many miracles. Many people were shocked by the power of the Holy Spirit. The blind received their sight, the lame walked, the sick were healed. All these were done during this evangelism ministry. We see how God's promise came into action. The prophet Joel had said it. We people of Vanuatu say "The Spirit of the Lord God is upon us because he has anointed us to preach the Gospel to the poor people of Vanuatu." Praise God for what he has done.

In where I live, in my poor home, I also started a home cell prayer group. Our goal is that the revival must come in the church. Please pray for me and also for the group. Our prayer group usually meets on Sunday night, after the night meeting. We started at 10:30 p.m. to 1 or 3.30 a.m. If we come closer to God he will also come close to us. We spent more time in listening and responding to God.

These revival movements continue to increase in the Pacific, especially as indigenous teams minister in other areas with the Spirit's fire. The Church grows stronger, even through opposition. Indigenous Christians live and minister in New Testament patterns from house to house and from village to village.

## 1965

*September 26—Soe, Timor (Mel Tari)*

The Spirit of God brought revival to Indonesia during the troubled and politically uncertain times there in the 1960's. Much of it happened outside the established church with a later acceptance of it in some churches. Thousands of Muslims were converted, the biggest Christian impact on Islam in history.

It started when a Bible School in East Java experienced revival with deep repentance, confession, renunciation of occult practices, burnings of fetishes and amulets, and a new humility and unity among staff and students. The Lord led individual students and teams in powerful evangelism in many islands.

A team visited Timor and saw evidences of revival beginning, which burst into unprecedented power in September 1965. This revival spread in the uncertain days following the attempted army coup on September 30, 1965, in Indonesia. Four days previously a visitation from God had begun in Timor at Soe, a mountain town of about 5,000 people.

A rebellious young man had a vision of the Lord who commanded him to repent, burn his fetishes, and confess his sins in church, the Reformed Church in Soe. He did, on Sunday, September 26, 1965, and he challenged others to do the same. Hundreds did.

That night, as at Pentecost, people heard the sound of a tornado wind and flames on the church building, which prompted police to set off the fire alarm to summon volunteer firefighters. Crowds came running to put out the fire, but the church was not burning. Many were converted that night, and many were filled with the Spirit and spoke in tongues. Some who did not know English spoke in English. By midnight, teams of lay people had been organized to begin spreading the gospel the next day.

Eventually, about 90 evangelistic teams were formed, which functioned powerfully with spiritual gifts.

The young man who testified that night in the church chose 23 young people who formed an evangelistic group, Team 1. They gave themselves full time to visiting churches and villages and saw thousands converted with multitudes healed and delivered. In one town, alone, they saw 9,000 people converted in two weeks.

Another young man, Mel Tari, witnessed this visitation of God and later became part of Team 42. He reported on this revival in two widely read books. Healings and evangelism increased dramatically. Specific directions from the Lord led the teams into powerful ministry with thousands becoming Christians. They saw many healings and miracles, such as water being turned to non-alcoholic wine for communion; they saw some instantaneous healings, deliverance from witchcraft and demonic powers, and raising people from death through prayer.

The teams were often guided supernaturally through provision of light at night on jungle trails; angelic guides and protection; the multiplication of meager supplies of food in pastors' homes when a team ate together during famines; and conversion of witchdoctors who saw power encounters when the teams' prayers banished demons, rendering the witchdoctors powerless.

The teams learned to listen to the Lord and obey Him. His leadings came in many biblical ways:

1. God spoke audibly, as with Samuel or Saul of Tarsus.

2. Many had visions, as did Mary or Cornelius.

3. There were inspired dreams, such as Jacob, Joseph, or Paul saw.

4. Prophecies, as in Israel and the early Church, occurred.

5. The still small voice of the Spirit led many, as with Elijah or Paul's missionary team.

6. The Lord often spoke through specific Bible verses.

7. Circumstances proved to be God-incidences not just coincidences.

8. Often when leadings were checked with the group or the church, the Lord gave confirmations and unity, as with Paul and Barnabas at Antioch.

The Reformed Church Presbytery on Timor recorded 80,000 conversions in the first year of the revival there, half of those being former communists. They noted that some 15,000 people had been permanently healed in that year. After three years the number of converts had grown to over 200,000. In those three years, over 200 evangelistic teams were formed. On another island where there had been very few Christians, 20,000 became believers in the first three years of the revival.

So often in times of great tribulation, political upheaval, and bloodshed, the Spirit of the Lord moves most powerfully and the Church grows most rapidly, as happens in many countries today.

## 1970

### *February 3—Wilmore, Kentucky (Asbury College)*

A revival broke out in Asbury College in Wilmore, Kentucky, on Tuesday, February 3, 1970. During the regular morning chapel, which commenced at 10 a.m., God moved on the students in such a way that many came weeping to the front to kneel in repentance, others gave testimonies including confession of sin, and all this was mixed with spontaneous singing. Lectures were canceled for the day as the auditorium filled with more than 1,000 people. Few left for meals. By midnight, over 500 still remained, praying and worshiping. Several hundred committed their lives to Christ that day. By 6 a.m. the next morning, 75 students were still praying in the chapel, and throughout Wednesday it filled again as all lectures were again canceled for the day. The time was filled with prayer, singing, confessions, and testimonies.

As they continued in prayer that week, many students felt called to share what was happening with other colleges and churches. Invitations began coming from around the country as news of the revival spread. So the next weekend, teams went out to tell the story and give their testimonies. Almost half the student body of 1,000 was involved in the teams witnessing about the revival.

In the first week after the revival began, teams of students visited 16 states by invitation and saw several thousand conversions through their witnessing. After six weeks, over 1,000 teams had gone from the college to witness, some of these into Latin America with finances provided by the home churches of the students. In addition, the adjacent Theological Seminary sent out several hundred teams of their students who had also been caught up in this revival.

Those remaining at the college prayed for the teams and gladly heard their reports on their return. The Holy Spirit moved in similar ways wherever they went. So the revival spread. The college remained a focus for the revival with meetings continuing at night and weekends, along with spontaneous prayer groups meeting every day. Hundreds of people kept coming to the college to see this revival and participate in it. They took reports and their own testimonies of changed lives back to their churches or colleges and so shared in the spread of the revival.

In the early 1970's, revival also spread among the hippie dropouts. Thousands were converted in mass rallies on the beaches and in halls, and they developed their own Jesus People magazines, music, and evangelism.

### August 23—Solomon Islands and the Pacific (Muri Thompson)

Muri Thompson, a Maori evangelist from New Zealand, visited the Solomon Islands in July and August 1970 where the church had already experienced significant renewal and was praying for revival. Many of these Christians were former warriors and cannibals gradually won to Christ in spite of initial hostility and the martyrdom of early missionaries and indigenous evangelists.

Beginning at Honiara, the capital, Muri Thompson spent two months visiting churches and centers on the islands. The national leaders and missionaries experienced deep conviction and repentance, publicly acknowledging their wrong attitudes. It was very humbling. A new unity and harmony transformed their relationships, and little things that destroyed that unity were openly confessed with forgiveness sought and given.

Then in the last two weeks of these meetings, the Holy Spirit moved even more powerfully with more deep repentance and weeping, sometimes even before the visiting team arrived. That happened on Sunday morning, August 23, 1970, on the island of Malaita; the whole congregation was deeply moved, and many were crying even before the team arrived from their berth in the ship, the *Evangel*, which carried the mission team of 40 people.

That Sunday morning, Muri Thompson preached powerfully. Then he said, "If anyone wants to come forward..." and immediately the whole congregation of 600 surged forward across the dirt floor under the thatched-leaf roof. Most of the people, including the pastors, cried with loud sobs of repentance, which soon gave way to outbursts of joy. Many saw visions of God, of Jesus on the cross or on His throne, of angels, or of bright light. Some spoke in tongues. Some were healed. Most came into a new experience of God with a deep awareness of the need for humility and sensitivity to the Holy Spirit.

The following Thursday, August 27, at another village on Malaita, the team found a people well prepared through many weeks of repentance, unity, and a growing longing to be filled with the Spirit. After preaching, Muri Thompson asked for a time of silent prayer, and the 2,000 people bowed in prayer. Then he heard a growing sound. At first he thought it was audible prayer from the congregation, but then he realized it came from above them, like wind getting louder. He said:

> I looked up through an opening in the leaf roof to the heavens from where the sound seemed to be coming. It grew to be roar—then it came to me: surely this is the Holy Spirit coming like a mighty rushing wind. I called the people to realize that God the Holy Spirit was about to descend upon them (Griffiths 1977, 175).

Three praying leaders in a nearby prayer house heard the silence and then the roaring sound. They came outside and heard it coming from immediately above the church. In the church people broke into wailing, praying, and strong crying. Conviction of sin increased, followed by deliverance and great joy. Weeping turned to joyful singing. Everywhere, people were talking about what the Lord had done to them. Many received healing and deliverance from bondage to evil spirits. Marriages were restored and young rebels transformed.

Everywhere people prayed together every day. They had a new hunger for God's Word. People responded quickly to the Spirit and wanted to be transparently honest and open with God and one another.

Normal lectures in the South Seas Evangelical Church Bible School were repeatedly abandoned as the Spirit took over the whole school with times of confession, prayer, and praise.

Teams from these areas visited other islands, and the revival spread. Eventually, pastors from the Solomon Islands visited other Pacific countries and saw similar moves of God there.

During September 1973, pastors from the Solomon Islands visited Enga Baptist churches in the highlands of New Guinea. They conducted meetings throughout the area, including sessions with village pastors. Revival broke out in many villages on Sunday, September 16, 1973, when the pastors returned to their churches. Hundreds of people, deeply convicted of sin, repented and were reconciled to God and one another with great joy. Pastors in one area held a retreat from Monday to Wednesday in a forest that previously had been sacred for animistic spirit worship. Others joined the pastors there. Healings included a lame man enabled to walk, a deaf mute who spoke and heard, and a mentally deranged girl restored to sanity.

Normal work stopped as people by the thousands hurried to special meetings. Prayer groups met daily, morning and evening. Most villages established special places for prayer, such as groves near the village where people could go and pray at any time. In the following months thousands of Christians were restored and hundreds converted. The church grew in size and maturity.

This was followed by tough times in the 1980's, when tribal conflict, destruction, and bloodshed erupted. Revival often precedes hard times and equips God's people to endure, or even to suffer for Him.

Pastors from the Solomon Islands also spoke on revival at a pastors' and leaders' conference at Goroka in the highlands of Papua New Guinea. Diyos Wapnok, from the Baptist Mission area at Telefolmin, attended the conference. He heard God call his name three times in the night there and realized that the Lord was drawing his attention to some special challenge. Later, on Thursday afternoon, March 10, 1977, at Duranmin in the rugged Western Highlands where Diyos was the principal of the Sepik Baptist Bible College, he spoke to about 50 people, and they were all filled with the Holy Spirit and with great joy.

The students experienced a light brighter than day filling the room. Many simultaneously felt convicted of unconfessed sin and cried out for mercy and forgiveness. All became aware of the majesty, authority, and glory of God. Revival had come to Duranmin and the Sepik district. This glimpse of God's greatness gave a new dimension to the students' preaching. The movement spread beyond the churches to villages throughout the Sepik area. During the next three years over 3,000 new believers were baptized.

In the Sepik lowlands of northern Papua New Guinea, a fresh visitation of God burst on the South Seas Evangelical Churches on Easter 1984, sparked by Solomon Island pastors. It featured repentance, confession, weeping, and great joy. Stolen goods were returned or replaced, and wrongs made right.

Australian missionary, Ray Overend, reported:

> I was preaching to an Easter convention at a place called Walahuta during the recent Sepik revival in Papua New Guinea. The words the Lord gave us were from Isaiah 6.... After the last word of the message the whole church rose to its feet and clapped loudly—something completely new to me! I knew they were not applauding me. They were acknowledging to God in praise the truth of his Word. ... Then I sat down in the only spare little space in the overcrowded church and the whole congregation began to sing—one song after another....

> Many faces were lifted to heaven and many hands raised in humble adoration. The faces looked like the faces of angels. They were radiating light and joy. And then I noticed something. Right beside me was a man who had heard the Word and now he just watched those radiant faces lost in praise. Then he hung his head and began to sob like a child. He was ministered to. Demons were cast out. And he received the Lord Jesus right into his heart. Then he too began to clap in gentle joy.

But who was he? A pastor came over to tell me that he had been until this moment the leader of the Tambaran cult in the Walahuta area—that satanic cult of which the whole village lived in mortal fear—and traditionally the whole of the Sepik feared that cult (Overend 1986, 9-10).

The man who was second-in-charge of the Tambaran cult in that area was also converted that day while he was listening to the worship from a distance as God's love and power overcame him.

Revival began to move through the area, until eventually it impacted the main mission station at Brugam. Ray Overend wrote:

I will never forget June 14th, 1984. Revival had broken out in many churches around but Brugam itself, with many station staff and many Bible College and Secondary School students, was untouched. For a whole week from 8th June a well known preacher from New Zealand (Fred Creighton) had brought studies on "Life in Christ by the power of His Spirit". There was much very thorough teaching. On Tuesday afternoon in prayer I had a real peace that the Lord would break through in Brugam. Then early on Thursday night, the 14th, Judah Akesi, the Church Superintendent, invited some of us to his office for prayer. During that prayer time God gave him a vision. In the vision he saw many people bowed down in the front of the church building in the midst of a big light falling down from above just like rain.

So after the ministry of the Word that night Judah invited those who wanted to bring their whole heart and mind and life under the authority of Christ to come forward so that hands might be laid on them for prayer.

About 200 people surged forward. Many fell flat on their faces on the ground sobbing aloud. Some were shaking—as spiritual battles raged within. There was quite some noise....

The spiritual battles and cries of contrition continued for a long time. Then one after another in a space of about three minutes everybody rose to their feet, singing spontaneously as they rose. They were free. The battle was won. Satan was bound. They had made Christ their King! Their faces looked to heaven as they sang. They were like the faces of angels. The singing was like the singing of heaven. Deafening, but sweet and reverent" (Overend 1986, 36-37).

The whole curriculum and approach at the Bible School for the area changed. Instead of having traditional classes and courses, teachers worked with the school all day—from prayer times early in the morning, through Bible teaching followed by discussion and sharing times during the day, to evening worship and ministry. The school became a community, seeking the Lord together.

Churches that have maintained a strong biblical witness continue to stay vital and strong in evangelism and ministry, filled with the Spirit's power. Christians learn to witness and minister in spiritual gifts, praying, and responding to the leading of the Spirit.

Many received spiritual gifts they never had before. One such gift was the "gift of knowledge" whereby the Lord would show Christians exactly where fetishes of sanguma men were hidden. Now in Papua New Guinea sanguma men (who subject themselves to indescribable ritual to be in fellowship with Satan) are able to kill by black magic.... In fact the power of sanguma in the East Sepik province has been broken (Overend 1986, 23-24).

In 1986 a senior pastor from Manus Island came to the Sepik to attend a one-year pastors' course. He was filled with the Spirit. When he went with a team of students on outreach, they prayed for an injured child who couldn't walk. Later in the morning he saw her walking around the town. The revival had restored New Testament ministries to the church, which amazed that pastor because he had never seen that before the revival.

The impact of the Solomon Islands revival continues to be felt across the Pacific. More recently, teams from the Solomons have visited Australia just to pray for that nation. They believe that God has shown them a mighty revival is on the way there also.

## 1971

### *October 13—Saskatoon, Canada (Bill McCleod)*

Wilbert (Bill) McLeod, a Baptist minister in his mid-50's, had often seen many people healed in answer to prayer, as he prayed with a group of deacons. He once anointed a woman with oil and prayed with her when she was dying of cancer. While he prayed, the woman had a vision of Jesus coming to her and touching her. She was healed.

Bill McLeod invited the twin evangelists, Ralph and Lou Sutera, to speak at his church in Saskatoon. Revival broke out with their visit, which began on Wednesday, October 13, 1971. By the weekend an amazing spirit gripped the people. Many confessed their sins publicly. The first to do so were the 12 counselors chosen to pray with inquirers. Numbers grew rapidly until the meetings had to be moved to a larger church building and then to the Civic Auditorium, which seated 2,000.

The meetings lasted many hours. People did not want to leave. Some stayed for a later meeting, called the Afterglow. Here people received prayer and counsel from the group as they continued to worship God and pray together. Humble confession of sin and reconciliations were common. Many were converted.

Taxi drivers became amazed that people were getting cabs home from church late into the night or early into the morning. Others were calling for taxis to take them *to* church late into the night as they were convicted by the Lord. Young people featured prominently. Almost half those converted were young. They gave testimonies of lives cleaned up by God and of restored relationships with their families. The atmosphere in schools and colleges changed from rebellion and cheating to cooperation, with many Bible study and prayer groups forming in the schools and universities.

Criminals confessed their sins and gave themselves up to the police. Restitution was common. People paid long overdue bills. Some businesses opened new accounts to hold the conscience money being paid to them. Many who cheated at restaurants or hotels returned to pay their full bill. People gave back stolen goods.

Christians found a new radical honesty in their lives. Pride and jealousies were confessed and transformed into humility and love. As people prayed for one another with new tenderness and compassion, many experienced healings and deliverance.

Yet, not all welcomed the revival. Some churches remained untouched by it or hostile to it. This seems common to all revivals.

Sherwood Wirt, then editor of the Billy Graham Association's magazine, *Decision*, reported:

> One day late in 1971 I read a strange report from Canada. Curious things were taking place in some congregations in the western provinces. Brothers and sisters, it was said, had been reconciled to each other; shop-lifted articles had been returned; crimes were being reported by the culprits; church feuds were being resolved; pastors were confessing their pride.

> But then I heard this word: "We're walking knee-deep in love up here" (Wirt 1975, 23).

In November a team went to Winnepeg and told of the revival at a meeting for ministers. The Holy Spirit moved powerfully, and many broke down confessing their sins. Rivalries and jealousies were confessed and forgiven. Many went home to put things right with their families. The ministers took this fire back into their churches, and the revival spread there also with meetings going late into the night as numbers grew and hundreds were converted or restored.

Sherwood Wirt reported on Bill McLeod's preaching at Winnepeg:

> I confess that what I saw amazed me. This man preached for only fifteen minutes, and he didn't even give an invitation! He announced the closing hymn, whereupon a hundred people came out of their seats and knelt at the front of the church. All he said was, "That's right, keep coming!"

> Many were young. Many were in tears. All were from the Canadian Midwest, which is not known for its euphoria. It could be said that what I was witnessing was revival. I believe it was (Wirt 1975, 46).

Bill McLeod and a team of six brought the revival to eastern Canada when they were invited to speak at the Central Baptist Seminary in Toronto. The meeting there began at 10 a.m. and went through until 1:15 a.m. Dinner was canceled, as no one wanted to leave. They did stop for supper, then went on again.

When the Sutera brothers commenced meetings in Vancouver on the Canadian West Coast on Sunday, May 5, 1972, revival broke out in the Ebenezer Baptist Church with 2,000 attending that first Sunday. The next Sunday 3,000 people attended in two churches. After a few weeks, five churches were filled.

The revival spread in many churches across Canada and into the northern United States, especially in Oregon. Everywhere, the marks of the revival included honesty before God and others with confession of sin and an outpouring of the love of God in those who repented. The German-speaking churches were also touched by the revival, and by May 1972 they chartered a flight to Germany for teams to minister there.

The Afterglow meetings were common everywhere in the revival. After a meeting had finished, those who wanted to stay on for prayer did so. Usually people desiring prayer knelt at a chair, and others laid hands on them and prayed for them. Many repented and were filled with the Spirit in the Afterglow meetings, which often went to midnight or later.

Sherwood Wirt reports on his experience of an Afterglow. As he sat in a chair, people came to pray for him. They told him to:

"Ask God to crucify you."

Crucify me? I wasn't even sure the idea was theologically sound.

"To do what?" I stammered.

"Nail you to the cross" was the reply....

"Now ask God to fill you with his Spirit and thank him for it...."

"You probably don't have much of a sensation of blessing now.... Don't worry. The feeling will come later—and how!"

She was right. It came. And it has never left....

The Holy Spirit used a divine solvent...to dissolve the bitterness in my heart.... In his own time and at his own pleasure he sent a divine solvent into this troubled heart. It was like the warmth of the sun burning off the layers of fog.

I don't know just how the love came in, but I know that all the bitterness I held against others—including those near to me—disappeared. Resentment—hostility—hurt feelings—you name it. They all dissolved. Evaporated. Went (Wirt 1975, 11-15).

He commented on this laying hands on people for prayer, which was normal in Afterglows: "Call it revival, renewal, a fresh touch, an anointing, times of refreshing, or what you will. I needed it" (Wirt 1975, 127).

That deep work of the Spirit continues now across the world. Its expressions vary with different cultures and denominational traditions. However, the divine Spirit deeply impacts those who continue to seek the Lord.

## 1973

*September 28—Phnom Penh, Cambodia (Todd Burke)*

In September 1973 Todd Burke arrived in Cambodia on a one-week visitor's visa. Just 23 years old, he felt a strong call from God to minister there, the only charismatic missionary in the country. Beginning with two English classes a day conducted through an interpreter, he taught from the Good News Bible. Those interested in knowing more about Jesus stayed after class; he saw regular conversions and people filled with the Spirit and healed. Revival broke out in the war-torn capital of Phnom Penh and rapidly spread to surrounding areas.

During that September, Todd's wife DeAnn joined him, and their visas were extended. A capable interpreter, Thay, joined their team, and they received government permission to hold a crusade in the athletic stadium, on Friday to Sunday afternoons, September 28-30. A singing team from the States arrived the day before the crusade began and led each meeting for half an hour with songs and testimonies.

Todd describes that first meeting:

About five thousand people were in the audience, most of them middle and lower class people. Among them was a large number of refugees. Seated to my left was a whole section of soldiers dressed in battle fatigues. Many of them had been wounded or had suffered the loss of a limb and I was touched by the look of hope written on their attentive faces. Before the meeting I overheard a reporter interviewing one soldier who was leaning on crutches near the platform. He had lost his right leg in combat. "I don't understand what this is going to be about," he said, "but maybe this Jesus can help to relieve our pain and sorrows." That was my prayer too....

As the time drew near for me to speak, I began praying for God to anoint me with the Holy Spirit. I needed his power to proclaim the Lordship of Jesus to these people who had never heard his message....

Thay was interpreting phrase by phrase and we seemed to have the people's attention. "I can't prove to you that Jesus offers more than you have in Buddha or in any other religion. Only Jesus can prove that to you as he did in the days when he walked the earth."

Then I began to relate the story of the paralytic man who had been healed by Jesus. During Thay's interpretation I prayed silently that the Holy Spirit would breathe life into those words and cause them to pierce each individual heart....

With a silent prayer (at the end of the message), I continued, "All of you who would like to know whether Jesus is Lord and has this power to save you and to heal you, please raise your hands." They went up all over the stadium; an air of restlessness crept over the crowd. "Now," I shouted into the microphone, "put your other hand on the area of your body where you need a healing. Or place your hand upon your heart if you want to have your sins forgiven and to find a new life in Christ." ...

Slowly I prayed a simple prayer so Thay could interpret every word clearly. ... I felt a surging confidence that the Holy Spirit was doing a mighty work at that moment (Burke 1977, 22-25).

Todd invited those who had been healed to come forward and testify. After a brief pause, hundreds streamed forward. A lady who had been blind for many years testified that right after the prayer she could see. A lame man who had been carried into the meeting found that he could walk again. There were too many healings for everyone to testify.

Each afternoon the crowds increased, and so did the impact of God's Presence. American TV crews reporting the war were pulled in to film the final crusade. It was shown across America. Todd described the final meeting:

Nearing the end of the message, I noticed people were already moving toward the front. Why are they coming already? I wondered. Have they been healed while I was speaking? ...

Some were coming for prayer, but most of them had been healed already.

I quickly ended my message and prayed with the entire audience, as I had done the two preceding days. When Thay invited people to come to the front and testify of what God had done for them, the response was incredible. For several hours, hundreds of people streamed across the platform as we watched in amazement.

When the procession was finished, Thay asked the remaining audience whether they believed Jesus had proved himself to be the Lord. They roared their agreement and then applauded spontaneously. "How many of you want to receive Jesus as your Saviour and Master?" he asked. A sea of hands raised before us. Our students and workers moved into the crowd to pray and counsel with as many as they could reach, handing out tracts and gospel portions and instructing people where they could go to learn more about Jesus (Burke 1977, 32-33).

Healings, miracles, and deliverance from demonic powers were regular events, which attracted new converts who, in turn, were filled with the power of the Spirit and soon began witnessing and praying for others. Many of those saved and healed began home churches.

A powerful Church spread through a network of small house churches. Todd met with the leaders of these groups at early morning prayer meetings every day at 6 a.m. Most pastors were voluntary workers holding normal jobs. Some cycled in from the country and returned for work each morning.

When the country fell to the communists in 1975, the Burkes had to leave. They left behind an amazing Church anointed by the power of God before it was buried by going underground to survive. Thousands of those new Christians died in the killing fields of Cambodia. Revival often offers mercy and grace prior to times of devastation or destruction.

# Chapter Five

# Late Twentieth Century

## 1975

### *April—Gaberone, Botswana (Reinhard Bonnke)*

German missionary to Africa, Reinhard Bonnke, founded Christ For All Nations (CFAN), which now ministers to millions. Converted at nine, he had missionary zeal. As a teenager Reinhard saw Johannesburg in South Africa in a vision of a map of Africa. At 19 he headed off to the Bible College of Wales to train as a missionary, even though he couldn't speak English. Three months later he was preaching in English! There he learned practical principles of living by faith.

After a short pastorate in Germany, where he married Anna, they left for missionary service in Africa. Working as traditional missionaries from 1967 to 1974 in Maseru, the capital of the small landlocked country of Lesotho, they saw meager results.

Near the end of that time Reinhard's interpreter broke down during his message at a healing meeting one Sunday morning and sank weeping to the floor because of God's awesome Presence. Waiting for the interpreter to recover, Reinhard "heard" the Lord speak "words" that amazed him: *My words in your mouth are just as powerful as My words in My own mouth.*

The "voice" repeated the sentence. He "saw" it like a movie from Scripture—Jesus told the disciples to speak in faith and it would happen. "I suddenly realized that the power was not in the mouth—the power was in the Word," said Reinhard.

Then, when the interpreter had recovered enough to speak, as he was preaching, Reinhard "heard" the Spirit say, "Call those who are completely blind and speak the word of authority."

He did. About six blind people stood. He boldly proclaimed, "Now I am going to speak with the authority of God, and you are going to see a white man standing before you. Your eyes are going to open."

He shouted, "In the name of Jesus, blind eyes open!" It shocked everyone as his voice resonated loudly against the bare brick walls.

Then a woman's voice shrieked, "I can see! I can see!" She had been totally blind for years. The other blind people also saw. The place erupted in excited cheers. A woman handed her crippled boy through the milling crowd to Reinhard, who sensed the power of God on the boy and watched amazed as the boy's crippled legs shook and straightened. That boy was healed. The meeting went on for hours as people screamed, shouted, danced, and sang.

At the end of 1974, Reinhard relocated to Johannesburg and established Christ For All Nations. Early in January, when he was ill, he had a vision of Jesus similar to Joshua's vision (see Josh. 5:13-15). He wrote:

> I was very sick. I didn't think I would make it. I went to doctors. Nothing helped. I was crying to God: "Lord what are you doing? What is your plan?" One afternoon I retired to my study. A thirst for prayer came over me and I was hardly on my knees when I saw a most wonderful vision. I saw the son of God stand in front of me in full armour, like a general. The armour was shining like the sun and burning like fire. It was tremendous and I realised that the Lord of Hosts had come. I threw myself at His feet. I laughed and I cried...I don't know

for how long, but when I got up I was perfectly healed (Steele 1984, 55).

When Reinhard flew to Gaberone in Botswana to buy time on the radio, the Lord told him to hire the 10,000-seater sports stadium for a crusade. The local Pentecostal pastor who helped prepare for the crusade felt apprehensive. He had only 40 in his congregation!

The crusade in April 1974 with Reinhard's evangelist friend, Pastor Ngidi, started in a hall that could seat 800. On the first night 100 attended. Healings happened every night, and people fell to the floor, overwhelmed. That was new to Reinhard.

By the end of the first week 2,000 people were packed into the hall. So they moved into the stadium! Thousands attended. People were saved and healed every night, and over 500 people were baptized in water within two weeks.

One night in the stadium, the Holy Spirit urged Reinhard to pray for people to be baptized in the Holy Spirit. So he asked an African coworker to give a message on the Holy Spirit. About 1,000 people responded to the call to be baptized in the Spirit. As soon as they raised their hands, they all fell on the ground, shouting and praising God in new languages. Reinhard was amazed. He had never seen anything like that before. It continued to happen in his crusades.

Eventually Reinhard used an enormous tent that could seat 30,000 people. Some Christ For All Nations crusades in Africa have reached huge open-air crowds of 600,000 to 800,000 people. Always hundreds or thousands are saved, healed, and delivered as the power of God moves on the people.

## 1979

### *March 14—Elcho Island, Australia (Djiniyini Gondarra)*

The Lord poured out the Holy Spirit on Elcho Island in northern Australia on Wednesday, March 14, 1979. Djiniyini Gondarra was then the Uniting Church minister in the small

town of Galiwin'ku at the south of the island. He had been away
on holidays to Sydney and Brisbane, returning on the late afternoon Missionary Aviation Fellowship flight.

He was travel-weary and just wanted to unpack and get to
bed early. Many of the people, however, had been praying for
months, and especially every day while he had been away, so
they wanted to have prayer and Bible study with him in his
home. This is his account of that Pentecost among Australian
Aborigines in the Arnhem Land churches across the north of
Australia:

> After the evening dinner, we called our friends to come and
> join us in the Bible Class meeting. We just sang some hymns
> and choruses translated into Gupapuynu and into Djam-
> barrpuynu. There were only seven or eight people who were
> involved or came to the Bible Class meeting, and many of our
> friends didn't turn up. We didn't get worried about it.
>
> I began to talk to them that this was God's will for us to get to-
> gether this evening because God had planned this meeting
> through them so that we will see something of his great love
> which will be poured out on each one of them. I said a word of
> thanks to those few faithful Christians who had been praying
> for renewal in our church, and I shared with them that I too
> had been praying for the revival or the renewal for this church
> and for the whole of Arnhem Land churches, because to our
> heavenly Father everything is possible. He can do mighty
> things in our churches throughout our great land.
>
> These were some of the words of challenge I gave to those of
> my beloved brothers and sisters. Gelung, my wife, also shared
> something of her experience of the power and miracles that
> she felt deep down in her heart when she was about to die in
> Darwin Hospital delivering our fourth child. It was God's
> power that brought the healing and the wholeness in her body.
>
> I then asked the group to hold each other's hands and I began
> to pray for the people and for the church, that God would pour

out his Holy Spirit to bring healing and renewal to the hearts of men and women, and to the children.

Suddenly we began to feel God's Spirit moving in our hearts and the whole form of our prayer suddenly changed and everybody began to pray in the Spirit and in harmony. And there was a great noise going on in the room and we began to ask one another what was going on.

Some of us said that God had now visited us and once again established his kingdom among his people who have been bound for so long by the power of evil. Now the Lord is setting his church free and bringing us into the freedom of happiness and into reconciliation and to restoration.

In that same evening the word just spread like the flames of fire and reached the whole community in Galiwin'ku. Gelung and I couldn't sleep at all that night because people were just coming for the ministry, bringing the sick to be prayed for, for healing. Others came to bring their problems. Even a husband and wife came to bring their marriage problem, so the Lord touched them and healed their marriage.

Next morning the Galiwin'ku Community once again became the new community. The love of Jesus was being shared and many expressions of forgiveness were taking place in the families and in the tribes. Wherever I went I could hear people singing and humming Christian choruses and hymns! Before then I would have expected to hear only fighting and swearing and many other troublesome things that would hurt your feelings and make you feel sad.

Many unplanned and unexpected things happened every time we went from camp to camp to meet with the people. The fellowship was held every night and more and more people gave their lives to Christ, and it went on and on until sometimes the fellowship meeting would end around about midnight. There was more singing, testimony, and ministry going on. People did not feel tired in the morning, but still went to work.

Many Christians were beginning to discover what their ministry was, and a few others had a strong sense of call to be trained to become Ministers of the Word. Now today these ministers who have done their training through Nungilinya College have been ordained. These are some of the results of the revival in Arnhem Land. Many others have been trained to take up a special ministry in the parish.

The spirit of revival has not only affected the Uniting Church communities and the parishes, but Anglican churches in Arnhem Land as well, such as in Angurugu, Umbakumba, Roper River, Numbulwar and Oenpelli. These all have experienced the revival, and have been touched by the joy and the happiness and the love of Christ.

The outpouring of the Holy Spirit in Arnhem Land has swept further to the Centre in Pitjantjatjara and across the west into many Aboriginal settlements and communities. I remember when Rev. Rronang Garrawurra, Gelung and I were invited by the Warburton Ranges people and how we saw God's Spirit move in the lives of many people. Five hundred people came to the Lord and were baptised in the name of the Father, the Son, and the Holy Spirit.

There was a great revival that swept further west. I would describe these experiences like a wild bush fire burning from one side of Australia to the other side of our great land. The experience of revival in Arnhem Land is still active in many of our Aboriginal parishes and the churches.

We would like to share these experiences in many white churches where doors are closed to the power of the Holy Spirit. It has always been my humble prayer that the whole of Australian Christians, both black and white, will one day be touched by this great and mighty power of the living God" (Gondarra 1991, 17-19).

The Renewal Fellowship in Brisbane invited a team from Elcho Island to minister at a combined churches Pentecost weekend in 1992. More than 20 Aborigines paid their airfare to come, saying they rarely had such opportunities. When they were asked to pray for the whites responding after their messages, they said, "We don't know how to pray for whites. We haven't done that." They soon learned, and prayed with the faith and gracious insights typical for them. When asked why white churches did not invite Aborigines to minister to them and why the revival did not touch white churches, they replied softly, "You are too proud."

A small Aboriginal community of about 30 adults with their children live at the far northern end of Elcho Island, accessible by four-wheel drive vehicles over a 50-kilometer dirt track. That community has been praying daily for revival in Australia and across the world for over 20 years. They meet for prayer each morning, during the day, and again each evening.

The Spirit of the Lord continues to stir people to pray earnestly for revival all over the world. Never has there been so much prayer as now.

## 1979

### *May 13—Anaheim, California (John Wimber)*

In 1977 John Wimber began leading the fellowship of approximately 40 people, which had been started by his wife, Carol. It later became the headquarters of the Vineyard Christian Fellowships. John preached from Luke's Gospel and began to pray for healings with no visible results for nine months, although the worship and evangelism attracted many people. Then healings began to happen and became a regular part of Vineyard ministry.

John Wimber summarized their story:

Beginning some time in September of 1976, Bob Fulton, Carol Wimber, Carl Tuttle, along with others, began assembling at the home of Carl Tuttle's sister. The agenda was simple: praying, worshipping and seeking the Lord. By the time I came several months later, the Spirit of God was already moving powerfully. There was a great brokenness and responsiveness in the hearts of many. This evolved into what became our church on Mother's Day in 1977.

Soon God began dealing with me about the work of the Spirit related to healing. I began teaching in this area. Over the next year and a half God began visiting in various and sundry ways. There were words of knowledge, healing, casting out of demons, and conversions. Later we saw an intensification of this when Lonnie Frisbee came and ministered. Lonnie had been a Calvary Chapel pastor and evangelist, being used mightily in the Jesus People Movement. After our Sunday morning service on Mother's Day 1979, I was walking out the door behind Lonnie, and the Lord told me, "Ask that young man to give his testimony tonight." I hadn't even met him, though I knew who he was and how the Lord had used him in the past. That night, after he gave his testimony, Lonnie asked the Holy Spirit to come and the repercussions were incredible. The Spirit of God literally knocked people to the floor and shook them silly. Many people spoke in tongues, prophesied or had visions.

Then over the next few months, hundreds and hundreds of people came to Christ as the result of the witness of the individuals who were touched that night, and in the aftermath. The church saw approximately 1,700 converted to Christ in a period of about three months.

This evolved into a series of opportunities, beginning in 1980, to minister around the world. Thus the Vineyard renewal ministry and the Vineyard movement were birthed (Wimber 1994, 1-3).

## 1979

### *July—Port Elizabeth, South Africa*
### *(Rodney Howard-Browne)*

Rodney Howard-Browne has seen hundreds of thousands converted through his ministry, and many more renewed in their love for the Lord and empowered by the Holy Spirit. His ministry remains controversial because of the manifestations involved, especially laughter.

In July 1979 when he was 18, Rodney Howard-Browne of Port Elizabeth, South Africa, attended an interdenominational prayer meeting with about 18 other young people. He had been desperately crying out to God, and at that meeting he prayed with the abandonment of youth, "God, either You come down here tonight and touch me, or I'm going to die and come up there and touch You."

He began shouting, "God, I want Your fire." After crying out for 20 minutes, suddenly he felt engulfed in the fire of God; he was totally overwhelmed, weeping, laughing, and praying in tongues. That continued for four days until he cried out, "God, lift it. I can't bear it any more.... Lord, I'm too young to die, don't kill me now."

For two weeks he felt that intense Presence of God. Then that intensity lifted for about ten years but later became common in his ministry.

In 1980, while he was ministering with a group of young people in a Methodist Church in South Africa, a woman in pain asked for prayer in the vestry before a service. He told what happened:

> I got up from my seat. I was going to put my hand on her head. And I lifted my hand and got it about here...like you'd pull a six-gun out of a holster and point it at somebody. And when my hand got about here, it felt like my fingertips came off, and out of my hand flowed a full volume of the anointing and the power of God, and it flowed right out of my hand and it went right in to her forehead and she crumbled in the floor. There was nobody in the room more amazed than me. And I looked down at the woman and I looked at my hand, and I'll tell you what—my hand—the fire of God—the anointing of God—the virtue—the *dunamis* was still coming out of my hand. It felt like my hand was a fire hose. And now you

start getting nervous—you think, I'd better look out where I point this thing. This thing's loaded now.

And so the rest of the team came in, and I didn't know what to do with it other than what we'd just done, so I said, "Lift your hands." ... Bam, they're all out in the back of the vestry. Now I'm in trouble. If the priest comes back, I'm finished. So I went around and just managed to get them just right and sober them up and say, "Get up and pull yourself together, we've got to go in to the meeting." We managed to get them all up except one girl. We had her propped between two men and got them out into the auditorium.

I get into the service, and that night I had to speak and I said to the Lord, "Lord, you know I'm not allowed to talk about Holy Ghost. You know I'm not allowed to talk about tongues. You know I'm not allowed to talk about 'fall' and 'power' and these words. Lord, how can we have what happened in the back room happen out here?" And the Lord said to me, "Call all those that want a blessing." Everyone raised their hands. So I said, "All right, get up, come up, and line up." And so I was going to go down and lay my hands on the first person's head. And the Lord said to me, "Just be very careful, and so don't put your hands on them because some people [will] think you'll push them over if you do." I take my finger, put it on the forehead of the first person and I said, "In the name of Jesus...." It looked like an angel stood there with a baseball bat and smacked them up the side of their head. And the person hit the floor. And I went down the line. Bam, Bam, Bam, Bam. The whole row was out under the power of God. Some of the people were pinned to the floor...for an hour and a half. Some of them, the moment they hit the ground they were speaking with other tongues, and we had said nothing about it. And that anointing stayed again for a period of two weeks.

Let me tell you right now—for an eighteen-year-old to experience that kind of anointing—it's dangerous. And then suddenly, it was gone. I prayed for people, they would fall down, but it was not the same. And I thought I'd lost the anointing.

So now I'm starting to pray—to get before God and find out: "What have I done to lose the anointing, and what formula must I use to get it back?" He said, "You can't do anything to get that anointing back. That anointing is not you. That anointing is all me. It has nothing to do with you." He said, "I just gave you a taste of what will come later on in your ministry, if you are faithful." He said, "If I gave it to you now, you'd destroy yourself. I can't give it to you now. There's no formula for it. If there was a formula for it, you'd do it and you'd get it, and you'd think it was you. From now on, whenever that anointing comes, you'll know it's not you and you'll know it's all me and you'll have to give me all the glory and all the praise and all the honour" (Riss 1995, Internet).

Rodney Howard-Browne moved to the United States in 1987 for evangelistic work. Then in April 1989 in Clifton Park, near Albany in upstate New York, he experienced powerful impacts of the Spirit during his meetings. He described it this way:

The power of God fell in the place without warning suddenly. People began to fall out of their seats, rolling on the floor. The very air was moving. People began to laugh uncontrollably while there wasn't anything funny. The less I preached, the more people were saved (Riss 1995, Internet).

His influence soon reached worldwide proportions, with hundreds being saved in his meetings and thousands being overwhelmed in many ways.

One example, which has now been repeated in many ways, is how revival touched the Christian Teaching and Worship Centre (CTWC) in Woburn, Boston, in November 1993. Mona Johnian and her husband, Paul, lead the 450-member church.

Revival broke out in their church after they attended revival meetings led by Rodney Howard-Browne in Jekyll Island Georgia, in November of 1993. At first, Mona was not impressed by the various phenomena she observed there, but she was surprised that her own pastor, Bill Ligon of Brunswick, Georgia, fell to the floor when Rodney Howard-Browne laid his hands upon him. "Bill is the epitome of dignity, a man totally under control," she said. The first chapter of her book describes a meeting at her church in which revival broke out while Bill Ligon was there as a guest minister. From the Johnians' church, the revival spread to other churches, including Bath Baptist Church of Bath, Maine, pastored by Greg Foster.

In a video entitled Revival, produced in his church in August of 1994, Paul Johnian said, "We cannot refute the testimony of the Church. ... What is taking place here is not an accident. It's not birthed by man. It's by the Spirit of God. ... The last week in October of 1993, Mona and I went down to Georgia. We belong to a Fellowship of Charismatic and Christian Ministries International, and we went down there for the annual conference. And hands were laid on us. And we were anointed. And I'm just going to be completely honest with you. What I witnessed there in the beginning I did not even understand. I concluded that what was taking place was not of God...because there was too much confusion. ... I saw something that I could not comprehend with my finite understanding. And it was only when I searched the Scriptures and asked God to show me and to reveal truth to me that I saw that what was taking place in the Body of Christ was a sovereign move of the Almighty. And I, for one, wanted to humble myself and be a part of the sovereign move of the Almighty. And I came back. I really didn't sense any change within me. But I came back just believing God that He was going to be doing something different in our congregation" (Riss 1995, Internet).

That story has now been multiplied in various forms in thousands of churches touched by this current impact of the Spirit.

## 1988

### *August 4—Kambaidam, Papua New Guinea (Johan van Bruggen)*

Johan van Bruggen, a missionary at the Lutheran Evangelist Training Centre at Kambaidam near Kainantu in the Eastern Highlands of Papua New Guinea, wrote in his circulars:

Tuesday afternoon, 2 August 1988: I was by myself watching a video of Bill Subritzky, an Anglican Evangelist in New Zealand, who has been mightily blessed by the Lord with ministries of healing and of deliverance from demons. A large group of Anglican Christians had been baptised in the Holy Spirit and were on the point of receiving gifts of the Spirit. I watched quite unemotionally when Bill said: "I will mention the gifts slowly and then just let the Holy Spirit impress on your mind which gift(s) he will give you."

He had just started with the first one: Words of Wisdom—when suddenly I was surrounded by Divine Presence. When it started I wanted to run away, scared stiff! But back came the words: Don't hold back, do not fear! So I stayed and said, "Come Holy Spirit, fill me completely." Now I know what it is to be drunk in the Spirit. I couldn't stand on my feet. I slumped on the bed, hands raised, trembling all over, tingling all over. I felt something moving up my gullet and I just said, "Out, out," and I literally threw up. Don't worry, I didn't make a mess. I just got rid of the spirit of fear and doubt! And oh, I felt absolutely fantastic. I cried and laughed and I must have been quite a sight! It rained hard and that rain was a solid muffler! Nobody knew. I came around again because there was the noise of the video set with a blank screen. The programme was finished and I did not know how. I have had earlier fillings of the Holy Spirit but nothing like this time with that sense of being overwhelmed.

Then came Thursday 4 August, a miserable day weather wise, although we had great joy during our studies. Evening devotions—not all students came, actually a rather small group. I too needed some inner encouragement to go as it was more comfortable near the fire. We sang a few quiet worship songs. Samson, a fellow who by accident became one of our students last year, well, this Samson was leading the devotions. We had sung the last song and were waiting for him to start. Starting he did, but in an unusual way. He cried, trembled all over! ... Then it spread. When I looked up again I saw the head prefect

flat on the floor under his desk. I was praying in tongues off
and on. It became quite noisy. Students were shouting! Should
I stop it? Don't hold back! It went on and on, with students
praying and laughing and crying—not quite following our
planned programme! We finally stood around the table, about
twelve of us, holding hands. Some were absolutely like drunk,
staggering and laughing! I heard a few students starting off in
tongues and I praised the Lord. The rain had stopped, not so
the noise. So more and more people came in and watched!

Not much sleeping that night! They talked and talked! And
that was not the end. Of course the school has changed completely. Lessons were always great, I thought, but have become greater still. Full of joy most of the time, but also with a
tremendous burden. A burden to witness....

What were the highlights of 1988? No doubt the actual outpouring of the Holy Spirit must come first. It happened on August 4 when the Spirit fell on a group of students and staff,
with individuals receiving the baptism of the Holy Spirit on
several occasions later on in the year. The school has never
been the same again. As direct results we noticed a desire for
holiness, a hunger for God's Word which was insatiable right
up till the end of the school year, and also a tremendous urge
to go out and witness. Whenever they had a chance many of
our students were in the villages with studies and to lead Sunday services. Prayer life deepened, and during worship services we really felt ourselves to be on holy ground....

We have been almost left speechless by what God is doing
now through our students. We realize that we have been led on
and are now on the threshold of a revival (van Bruggen 1989).

David, a young student in his early twenties from the Mark-
ham Valley, had a growing burden for his area of Ragizaria and
Waritzian, known and feared for its pagan occult practices. He
prayed earnestly. As part of an outreach team he visited nearby
villages and then went to his own people. He was concerned

about the low spiritual life of the church. He spent a couple of days alone praying for them.

One Saturday night he was invited to lead the village devotions at Ragizaria. Johan van Bruggen told the story in his circulars:

Since most of the Ragizaria people are deeply involved in witchcraft practices, David made an urgent appeal for repentance. Two men responded and came forward. David put his hands on them and wanted to pray, when suddenly these two men fell to the ground. They were both praising the Lord. Everybody was surprised and did not know what to think of this. David himself had been slain in the Spirit at Kambaidam in August 1988, but this was the first time that this had happened to others through him. The next morning during the Sunday service scores of people were slain in the Spirit. Said David, "People entered the church building and immediately they were seized by God's power. They were drunk in the Spirit and many could not keep standing. The floor was covered with bodies. It did not only happen to Lutherans, but also to members of a Seventh Day Adventist congregation (former Lutherans) that were attracted by the noise and commotion."

David reported that there was a sense of tremendous joy in the church and people were praising the Lord. Well, the service lasted for hours and hours. Finally David said, "And now the people are hungry for God's Word and not only in my village, but also in Waritzian, a nearby village. And they want the students to come with Bible studies. Can we go next weekend?"

We all felt that some students together with Pastor Bubo should go....

Pastor Bubo told me, "Acts 2 happened all over again!" For three days all the people were drunk in the Spirit. God used the students and Bubo in a mighty way. On Saturday night the Holy Spirit was poured down on the hundreds of people that had assembled there. From then on until the moment the school car arrived on Monday noon, the people were being filled again and again by the Spirit. There was much rejoicing. There were words of prophecy. There was healing and deliverance. And on Monday morning all things of magic and witchcraft were burned. Everybody was in it, the leaders, the young, yes even little children were reported to be drunk in the Spirit. ... The people did not want to go and sleep, saying, "So often we have had drunken all-night parties. Now we will have a divine party until daybreak."

This area had been a stronghold of evil practices. Many people received various spiritual gifts including unusual abilities such as speaking English in tongues and being able to read the Bible. People met for prayer, worship and study every day and at night. These daily meetings continued to be held for over two years (van Bruggen 1989).

In November 1990, Johan van Bruggen wrote:

This is what happened about two months ago. A new church building was going to be officially opened in a village in the Kainantu area. Two of our last year's graduates took part in the celebrations by acting the story in Acts 3: Peter and John going to the temple and healing the cripple.

Their cripple was a real one—a young man, Mark, who had his leg smashed in a car accident. The doctors had wanted to amputate it, but he did not want to lose his useless leg. He used two crutches to move around the village. He could not stand at all on that one leg. He was lying at the door of the new church when our Peter and John (real names: Steven and Pao) wanted to enter. The Bible story was exactly followed: "I have got no money, but what I have I give you. In the name of Jesus Christ of Nazareth, rise up and walk!" Well, they acted this out before hundreds of people, among them the president of the Goroka Church District and many pastors and elders. Peter (Steven) grabbed the cripple (Mark) by the hand and pulled him up. And he walked! He threw his crutches away and loudly praised the Lord! Isn't that something? What a faith!

Their testimony was given at a meeting of elders when Kambaidam was discussed. Mark was a most happy fellow who stood and walked firmly on his two legs. He also had been involved in criminal activities, but in this meeting he unashamedly confessed his faith in the Lord Jesus.

Later I talked with them. Steven (Peter) told me that the Lord had put this on his heart during a week-long period of praying. "I had no doubt that the Lord was going to heal Mark, and I was so excited when we finally got to play-act!" And Mark? He told me that when Steven told him to get up he just felt the power of God descend upon him and at the same time he had a tingling sensation in his crippled leg: "I just felt the blood rushing through my leg, bringing new life!" Mark is now involved in evangelistic outreach and his testimony has a great impact (van Bruggen 1989).

## 1988

### *Madruga, Cuba*

In 1988, revival broke out in a small church in Madruga, Cuba. "People would begin to weep when they entered the church," said their pastor. More than 60 churches experienced a similar move of the Spirit. And today the Holy Spirit's Presence is still being felt. Despite gestures of tolerance towards Christians, believers in Cuba still experience much hardship and oppression. Nevertheless, God is moving among the ten million people of Cuba, just as in the early Church.

The revival produced more than 2,400 house churches—more than all the official churches put together. Though open evangelism is still outlawed, teenagers were joining the children and adults to witness boldly in parks, beaches, and other public places, regardless of the risk.

There is a "holy and glorious restlessness" among the believers, said one pastor. "The once defensive mood and attitude of the church has turned into an offensive one, and

Christians are committed to the vision of 'Cuba Para Cristo!'—
Cuba for Christ!'" (*Open Doors*, Australian circular, September
1993, 1-2)

Cubans saw astounding revival from 1988. The Pentecostals, Baptists, independent evangelical churches, and some
Methodist and Nazarene churches experienced it. One Assemblies of God church had approximately 100,000 visit it in six
months, often in bus loads. One weekend they had 8,000 visitors, and on one day the four pastors (including two youth pastors) prayed with over 300 people.

In many Pentecostal churches the lame walked, the blind
saw, the deaf heard, and many people's teeth were filled. Often
2,000 to 3,000 attended meetings. In one evangelical church
over 15,000 people accepted Christ in three months. A Baptist
pastor reported signs and wonders occurring continuously with
many former atheists and communists testifying to God's
power. So many were converted that churches could not hold
them; they met in various house churches.

In 1990, an Assemblies of God pastor in Cuba with a small
congregation of less than 100 people meeting once a week suddenly found he was conducting 12 services a day for 7,000 people. They started waiting in line at 2 a.m. and even broke down
doors just to get into the meetings (Robinson 1992, 14).

## 1989

### *Henan and Anhul, China*

Dennis Balcombe, pastor of the Revival Christian Church in
Hong Kong, regularly visits China. He has reported on revival
there.

In 1989 Henan preachers visited North Anhul province and
found several thousand believers in the care of an older pastor
from Shanghai. At their first night meeting with 1,000 present,
30 were baptized in the icy winter. The first baptized was a lady
who had convulsions if she went into water. She was healed of

that and other ills, and found the water warm. A 12-year-old boy who was deaf and dumb was baptized and spoke, "Mother, Father, the water is not cold—the water is not cold." An aged lady nearly 90, disabled after an accident while in her 20's, was completely healed in the water. By the third and fourth nights over 1,000 were baptized.

A young evangelist, Enchuan, 20 years old in 1990, had been leading evangelistic teams since he was 17. He said, "When the church first sent us out to preach the Gospel, after two to three months of ministering we usually saw 20-30 converts. But now it is not 20. It is 200, 300, and often 600 or more will be converted."

Sister Wei, 22 years old in 1991, spent 48 days in prison for leading open-air worship. She saw many healings in prison and many conversions.

On March 12, 1991, *The South China Morning Post* acknowledged there were a million Christians in central Henan province, many having made previously unheard of decisions to voluntarily withdraw from the Communist party. "While political activities are cold-shouldered, religious ones are drawing large crowds" (Balcombe 1991, 1-2).

Dennis Balcombe reported in a newsletter on August 27, 1994:

> This year has seen the greatest revival in Chinese history. Some provinces have seen over 100,000 conversions during the first half of this year. Because of this, the need for Bibles is greater than ever. This year we have distributed to the house churches over 650,000 New Testaments, about 60,000 whole Bibles, one million Gospel booklets and thousands of other books (Balcombe 1994, 1-2).

Revival continues in China with mighty signs and wonders amid severe persecution, just as in the early Church.

## Chapter Six

# Final Decade, Twentieth Century[1]

## 1992

### *Buenos Aires, Argentina (Claudio Freidzon)*

Karin Detert of Berlin, Germany, reported on revival in Argentina.

The prelude to these events was in the early 1980s, at which time God raised up Carlos Annacondia, a businessman turned evangelist. Crowds gathered together to hear him preach because his ministry was accompanied by signs and wonders, healings (for instance, filling of teeth) and deliverances. In mass crusades thousands of people accepted Christ as Saviour. Virtually every church grew.

In 1992, a second wave of revival began with Claudio Freidzon, founder of a Buenos Aires church that in four years

---

1. Historian Richard Riss gathered many reports of current revivals in his article, "A History of the Worldwide Awakening of 1992-1995." He has kindly given permission to use his material, the full text of which is published on the Internet. Much of this chapter is drawn from that material.

has grown to 3000 people. Pastor Claudio, who was very busy in all areas of his church felt a need to really come to know the Holy Spirit. Whilst he was seeking an encounter with God, the Holy Spirit touched him one day in a powerful way and his ministry changed dramatically. An unusual presence of the Holy Spirit started accompanying him in his meetings.

During the services, as people entered into adoration and worship, some became drunk in the Spirit and could not stand up. Some had to be taken home by others because they could not drive or walk on their own. Others laughed in the Spirit or fell under the power of God. The services were very long (4-5 hours), many miraculous healings were reported. Other pastors came to see and to receive the same anointing. Claudio prayed for them and they received a fresh and new anointing and took it back to their churches.

A hallmark of this revival is an emphasis on worship and praise. God's presence descends as we immerse ourselves in adoring Him. Some people weep throughout an entire service; others rejoice with laughter. Many are led to deep repentance, pastors and congregation.

An emphasis on personal holiness has caused many to change their lifestyles. Less time spent watching television, for example. Critics have accused some of faking religious experiences. But the emphasis on holiness, the desire of the people to praise and worship, and increase in concern for reaching others with the Gospel are genuine. And although the revival started in Claudio's church, it has spread to hundreds of pastors and churches in Argentina.

God has also opened doors for a world-wide ministry and, wherever he goes he ministers in this same anointing, which then remains in those places; and so this revival could be brought to many other places around the world, like for instance, also to my own church in Berlin, where God started moving in a tremendous way since September, 1993, when Claudio came to minister in our church.

This new wave of the Holy Spirit started about two and a half years ago in Claudio's church and is still going on. I had the privilege of being part of their wonderful services where people were always caught up in a tremendous worship, sometimes weeping in the services, sometimes laughing. The presence of God was always very powerful. The people in the church are very healthy and spiritually strong in the Word. There is a bold emphasis on the need for balance between the Word and the Spirit" (Riss 1995).

How did this amazing ministry begin? Australian editor Robert McQuillan gathered reports to file this account:

When Argentina's Claudio Freidzon stood before a crowd of over 65,000 in Buenos Aires' Velez Sarsfield stadium it was like a dream come true. As a boy he had dreamed of becoming a professional soccer player; being a pastor had been the furthest thing from his mind. Now, walking onto the field for a gospel crusade, he had the wonderful opportunity of scoring a few goals against the devil! Six hours of revivalist fervour would see many salvations and Holy Spirit miracles, healings and manifestations.

Claudio Freidzon is among the foremost figures of the extraordinary revival that has been taking place in Argentina since 1992. He has also been a catalyst for the current worldwide revival—as the saying goes, "Before there was Toronto or Sunderland, there was Argentina." More than 850,000 people have attended his crusades. As well as many healings from a whole range of sicknesses, countless lives have been dramatically changed—restoration of families has been a highlight in this revival, children pray for one another, and youngsters prefer to visit hospitals rather than play ball.

But success did not come easily for Claudio. When he and his wife, Betty, commenced ministry they set up both church and home in the one usable room in a dilapidated building. At night they replaced the chairs with their bed and a cot for the children. Those trying days proved a desert experience for

Claudio which led him to a spiritual hunger and discovering complete dependence on the Holy Spirit. He says, "The only fountain is God himself. The only solution comes from heaven."

With a congregation of just seven for seven years, he was on the point of giving up. But God wouldn't let him. He recalls:

> Sometimes pastor friends came to visit and would find me alone in the meeting. I felt like dying: I wished I could disappear. I used to walk among the empty benches and the devil laughed and jumped around me, whispering in my ear: "You're no good; you'll never make any progress; it will always be like this."

> And unfortunately I believed him. One day I thought: "This isn't for me. I'm going to give up the pastorate. I'm going to resume my engineering studies and get myself a job." But deep down I knew that was not God's plan.

> I went and saw my superintendent for the purpose of handing in my credentials. But before I could tell him, he said, "Claudio, I have something to say to you. God has something to say to you. He has something wonderful for you. You don't see it, but God is going to use you greatly."

> He went on: "Look, I started in a very precarious house and had no help from anybody. Sometimes I had nothing to eat and I suffered greatly. But we prayed and God provided for each day and we felt grateful. I knew we were doing God's will. And when I think of you, Claudio, I know you are going to be useful to God and that you are within his will. I don't know what your problems are, but keep on. By the way, what brings you here today?"

> I put my credentials back in my pocket and said, "Well..., nothing in particular, I thought I would just come and share a moment with you." There was nothing else I could say. When I got home Betty was weeping and I said, "Betty, we're going to continue." I embraced her tightly and we started all over again.

Claudio Freidzon went on to hunger from the depths of his soul for the touch of God that would enable him to reach the masses. Desperate, and churning and aching inside as with hunger for natural food, Claudio desired and craved for the bread of life. He was to discover that heart attitude is of primary interest to God and that through developing our relationship with him, the Holy Spirit is free to inspire any committed Spirit-hungry Christian to do great exploits in Jesus' name.

In his search for more of God, Claudio Freidzon visited Orlando and requested that Benny Hinn pray for him. The evangelist did so, praying that the anointing of the Holy Spirit would rest on the Argentinian's life and ministry and that God would do a great work through him in that nation. The rest is history! Claudio Freidzon began holding incredible rallies, presenting the message of the transforming power of the Holy Spirit and revival swept the country. What began as a personal work of the Holy Spirit in his own life because of his spiritual hunger affected others. Today he pastors a prosperous church of over 4,000 members and is bringing spiritual life to hundreds of thousands both in Argentina and in other nations (McQuillan 1997, 46-48).

The revival ministries of Claudio Freidzon, Hector Giminez, Carlos Annacondia, and Omar Cabrera have won hundreds of thousands to the Lord. All of them have powerful ministries in evangelism with many signs and wonders, healings and miracles. Yet, not only do evangelists make an astounding impact on the nation, but ordinary people in hundreds and thousands are also praying for revival in Argentina and around the world.

Before the fire of God fell on their church in Toronto, Canada, John and Carol Arnott visited Argentina to seek a fresh touch from the Lord. Various leaders prayed for them, but so did converted prisoners. John Arnott reported:

In La Plata, near Buenos Aires, there is a maximum security prison for 4000 inmates. This prison was out of control, and basically run by gangs within the prison. But permission was given to hold meetings there. They had pastors who were given responsibility over the converts. This was under the auspices of Carlos Annacondia.

Over a period of five years, a Christian floor developed in the prison, of eight hundred people. This floor had round the clock prayer meetings, and 180 people were always praying at any given time, waiting before the Lord, and asking God to have mercy. Over the course of five years, 600 men completed their sentences, and only one was later re-arrested. Other prisoners always want to go to the Christian floor of the prison because it is safe and clean. They have corking on the bars to make things more comfortable. So others get saved as a result of going to the Christian floor. When they think they are ready, the prisoners apply to be transferred to another prison, and then start some of the same things in other prisons (Riss 1995).

Describing Argentina as a flashpoint of revival, C. Peter Wagner, wrote:

Like a burning, dry tinder, the Spirit of God has ignited an extraordinary spiritual bonfire in Argentina over the last ten years. From the southern tip of Tierra del Fuego (Land of Fire) to breathtaking Iguazu Falls in the northeast, the flames of revival have blazed through Argentina and beyond, making the country one of the flashpoints of church growth in the world today....

Argentine evangelist Carlos Annacondia began his crusade ministry in 1982, the year of Argentina's defeat in the Malvinas, just as the Spirit of God began to spark spiritual renewal. Since then, over a million and a half people have made public commitments to Christ during the course of Annacondia's ministry.

Hector Giminez was a drug addicted criminal when God called him into the Kingdom. He began ministering to troubled youth; and within a year, was leading a congregation of

1,000. Since 1986 his church in downtown Buenos Aires has exploded in size to over 120,000 members, making it the third largest church in the world.

The world's fourth largest church is also Argentina. Omar Cabrera and his wife Marfa began their ministry during the tough years of the 1970s. Long before most Argentine pastors, they began experiencing God's blessing as they learned the power of prayer to liberate people from sin, sickness, and the forces of evil. Now their church, centred in Santa Fe, ministers to 90,000 members in 120 cities.

The revival that began in the early 1980s has touched virtually every evangelical denomination.... The stirrings of revival have drawn Argentine Christians into unprecedented forms of unity. ACIERA, the national association of evangelical Christian churches, and the monthly evangelical tabloid *El Puente* (*The Bridge*) has helped believers focus on common goals" (Riss 1995).

Unprecedented unity, fervent prayer, and New Testament ministries of signs and wonders give Argentina's revival incredible worldwide impact now. Leaders from around the world visit such flash points of revival, catch the fire themselves, and ignite others as they preach and pray in the power of the Holy Spirit, just as Jesus taught the disciples to do.

## 1993

### *May 2—Brisbane, Australia (Neil Miers)*

Jill Austin from Kansas City in America spoke at the pastors' conference for Christian Outreach Centre in New Zealand in April 1993 where Neil Miers, the President of Christian Outreach Centre, also spoke.

Jill Austin is a part of the prophetic team at Metro Christian Fellowship. God has used her to impart His manifest Presence to congregations—to bring refreshment, prophetic vision, and proclamation, and to ignite the fires of God among them. That happened in New Zealand, causing drunkenness in the Spirit, visions, prophecies, laughter, tears, and people overwhelmed on the floor.

Neil and Nance Miers returned to Brisbane, Australia, their headquarters, to lead the national conference for their regional pastors. Neil preached at their headquarters church in Brisbane on Sunday night, May 2. Fire fell.

Darren Trinder, editor of their magazine, *A New Way of Living* (now *Outreach*), reported:

> Some staggered drunkenly, others had fits of laughter, others lay prostrate on the floor, still more were on their knees while others joined hands in an impromptu dance. Others, although showing no physical signs, praised the Lord anyway, at the same time trying to take it all in. People who had never prayed publicly for others moved among the crowd and laid hands on those present.

> "When we first saw it in New Zealand early in April we were sceptical," said Nance Miers, wife of Christian Outreach Centre International President, Pastor Neil Miers. "I've seen the Holy Spirit move like this here and there over the years. But this was different. In the past it seemed to have affected a few individuals, but this time it was a corporate thing."

> Neil Miers himself was physically affected, along with several other senior pastors, early in this Holy Ghost phenomenon. Later he viewed the series of events objectively. "It started in New Zealand and then broke out in New Guinea, and now it's here. If I know the Holy Ghost, it will break out across the world—wherever people are truly seeking revival. For the moment this is what God is saying to do, and we're doing it. It's that simple."

> But despite the informal nature of the events, Pastor Miers, adopting his shepherd role, was careful to monitor the situation. "There are some who are going overboard with it; just like

when someone gets drunk on earthly wine for the first time. The next time it happens they'll understand it a little better."

God is doing many things. He's loosening up the church. He's working deep repentance in certain individuals, and healing deep hurts in others. Just like the outpouring in Acts, it was the public ministry that followed which really changed the world. First God has to shake up the church and then He uses these people to shake up the world.

Splashes of this revival have touched people's lives throughout the Christian Outreach Centre movement around the nation and the world (Trinder 1994, 65-74).

This outpouring of the Spirit at Christian Outreach Centre in Brisbane affected people deeply for weeks. Office staff, when prayed for, were overwhelmed, so sometimes the phones rang unanswered. The Bible College canceled lectures as staff and students were powerfully affected, often "drunk in the Spirit." They had vivid visions and prayed for others constantly. Children in the primary and high schools were similarly overwhelmed, saw visions, and worshiped and prayed as never before. Many people now in full-time ministry were powerfully impacted then, and the Christian Outreach Centre movement continues to grow rapidly internationally with approximately 200 churches in Australia and over 350 overseas in 1997.

## 1994

### *January 20—Toronto, Canada (John Arnott, Randy Clark)*

John Arnott, senior pastor at the Toronto Airport Christian Fellowship (then called the Toronto Airport Vineyard Christian Fellowship) tells how the Father's blessing came to them in 1994:

In October 1992, Carol and I started giving our entire mornings to the Lord, spending time worshipping, reading, praying and being with him. For a year and a half we did this, and we fell in love with Jesus all over again....

We heard about the revival in Argentina, so we travelled there in November 1993 hoping God's anointing would rub off on us somehow. We were powerfully touched in meetings led by Claudio Freidzon, a leader in the Assemblies of God in Argentina. ... We came back from Argentina with a great expectation that God would do something new in our church.

We had a taste of what the Lord had planned for us during our New Year's Eve service as we brought in 1994. People were prayed for and powerfully touched by God. They were lying all over the floor by the time the meeting ended. We thought, "This is wonderful, Lord. Every now and then you move in power." But we did not think in terms of sustaining this blessing.

We invited Randy Clark, a casual friend and pastor of the Vineyard Christian Fellowship in St. Louis, Missouri, to speak because we heard that people were being touched powerfully by God when he ministered. We hoped that this anointing would follow him to our church.

Yet Randy and I were in fear and trembling, hoping God would show up in power, but uncertain about what would happen. We were not exactly full of faith—but God was faithful anyway.

On January 20, 1994, the Father's blessing fell on the 120 people attending that Thursday night meeting in our church. Randy gave his testimony, and ministry time began. People fell all over the floor under the power of the Holy Spirit, laughing and crying. We had to stack up all the chairs to make room for everyone. Some people even had to be carried out.

We had been praying for God to move, and our assumption was that we would see more people saved and healed, along with the excitement that these would generate. It never occurred to us that God would throw a massive party where people would laugh, roll, cry and become so empowered that emotional hurts from childhood were just lifted off them. The phenomena may be strange, but the fruit this is producing is extremely good (Arnott 1995, 58-59).

People were saved and healed, more in the next two years than ever before at that church. Other visitors experienced this renewal, discovering a new deep love for the Lord, which they then passed on to others.

Word spread. Thousands flew or drove to visit the little church at the end of the runway at Toronto International Airport. The church had to relocate into larger premises. The blessing still continues. British journalists nicknamed this renewal the "Toronto Blessing."

The impact of the Spirit in Toronto continues. Steve Long, a pastor at Toronto Airport Christian Fellowship, sent this e-mail message to John Arnott on August 29, 1996:

At the Intercession Prayer Meeting:

The Presence of God was particularly strong to-day and one gentleman came forward to share what I thought [would be what] God was saying to the Intercession Group, but actually he shared that he was put to sleep by the Holy Spirit in the meeting and when he woke up his back was completely healed. He shared that he had blown three discs in his back and he knows that he was healed. John, it turns out that he is a chiropractor. No one prayed for him. He shared his testimony at the evening service. Praise be to God! Perhaps the new paradigm is being ushered in with a new level of power and sovereign healings.

A Jewish mom and dad plus their daughter and her boyfriend were saved last night after being powerfully impacted by the Holy Spirit.

Salvation. Healing. Release from oppression. Weeping. Laughter. New zeal for the Lord. Leaders impacted by the Spirit of God finding their own churches similarly impacted. These results have been reported by hundreds of thousands of visitors to Toronto.

It is controversial. As with all strong moves of God's Spirit, people react in many ways. The media highlights anything unusual or strange. However, the vast majority of people prayed for at Toronto report profound blessing, and, in turn, bless others with their zeal for God.

John Arnott and teams from Toronto continue to ignite revival fires across America and around the world. For example, in January of 1995, John Arnott, as well as Wes Campbell of New Life Vineyard Fellowship in Kelowna, British Columbia, began speaking for two or three days each at Mott Auditorium on the campus of the U.S. Center for World Mission. By March 24 people gathered for meetings five nights a week, usually going very late. John Arnott conducted powerful meetings there on Friday-Sunday, March 24-26, hosted by Harvest Rock Church, a Vineyard Fellowship. Then the combined churches in the area continued with nightly meetings on Monday, March 27. Later that settled to meetings from Wednesday to Sunday each week. Then Wednesdays were reserved for cell groups, and meetings continued from Thursday to Sunday nights.

Che Ahn, senior pastor of Harvest Rock Church wrote in their monthly magazine, *Wine Press*, of August 1995:

> I am absolutely amazed at what God has done during the past five months. After John Arnott exploded onto the scene with three glorious and unforgettable renewal meetings, he encouraged the pastors of our church to begin nightly protracted meetings. My mind immediately rejected the idea. I thought to myself, "The meetings were great because you were here, but how can we sustain nightly meetings without someone like John Arnott to draw the crowd?" The answer to my question was an obvious one. Someone greater than John Arnott would show up each night at the meetings—Jesus. And each night since we began March 27, 1995, God has shown up to heal, to save, and to touch thousands of lives. There is no accurate way to measure the impact that the renewal meetings are having in our city. I do believe that we are making church history, and

we are in the midst of another move of the Holy Spirit that is sweeping the world. From March 27 to July 27, we have had 99 nightly renewal meetings. We have averaged about 300 people per night, some nights with more that 1200 people and others with a small crowd of 120.

More than 25,000 people have walked through the doors of Mott Auditorium, many of them happy, repeat customers. We have seen more that 300 people come forward to rededicate their lives or give their hearts to Jesus Christ. These statistics don't come close to representing other evangelistic fruit of those who have attended the meetings. For example, two church members, Justine Bateman and Jeff Eastridge, had an outreach at Arroyo High School and more than 60 young people gave their hearts to the Lord!

We have seen marvellous healings from the hand of the Lord, many of them spontaneous without anyone specifically praying for the healing. I wish I had the time and space to share all the wonderful fruit I have seen at the renewal meetings. Seeing the need to share what God is doing, I felt that we are producing this church newsletter to share these testimonies of lives that have been impacted by God during this current outpouring of the Holy Spirit" (Ahn 1995).

## 1994

### *May 29—Brompton, London (Eleanor Mumford)*

The Anglican Church, Holy Trinity Brompton (HTB), near Kensington in London, has been powerfully affected by the current awakening—and widely reported in the media.

Eleanor Mumford, assistant pastor of the South-West London Vineyard and wife of John Mumford (the pastor and the overseer of the Vineyard Churches in Britain), told a group of friends about her recent visit to the Toronto Airport Vineyard in Canada. When she prayed for them, the Holy Spirit profoundly affected them.

Nicky Gumbel, Curate of Holy Trinity Brompton, was there. He rushed back from this meeting with his wife, Pippa, to the HTB church office in South Kensington where he was late for a staff meeting. The meeting was ready to adjourn. He apologized, told what had happened, and was then asked to pray the concluding prayer. He prayed for the Holy Spirit to fill everyone in the room. The church newspaper, "HTB in Focus," June 12, 1994, reported the result:

> The effect was instantaneous. People fell to the ground again and again. There were remarkable scenes as the Holy Spirit touched all those present in ways few had ever experienced or seen. Staff members walking past the room were also affected. Two hours later some of those present went to tell others in different offices and prayed with them where they found them. They too were powerfully affected by the Holy Spirit— many falling to the ground. Prayer was still continuing after 5 pm (Riss 1995).

The church leaders invited Eleanor Mumford to preach at Holy Trinity Brompton the next Sunday, May 29, at both services. After both talks, she prayed for the Holy Spirit to come upon the people. Some wept. Some laughed. Many came forward for prayer and soon lay overwhelmed on the floor.

Cassette tapes of those services circulated in thousands of churches in England. A fresh awakening began to spread through the churches. These are some of Eleanor Mumford's comments:

> A Baptist pastor [Guy Chevreau] was involved in this remarkable move of the Spirit of God which seems to be taking place in eastern Canada. He's written this: "At meetings hosted by the Airport Vineyard, Toronto, there has come a notable renewal and revival of hope and faith and of expectation. Over the past eighteen weeks, now about 130 days consecutively, the Spirit of God has been pouring out freedom, joy, and power in the most remarkable ways. Six nights a week,"— because they take a day off for Monday, six nights a week— "between 350 and 800 people at a time gather for worship,

testimony and ministry. Rededications are numerous. Conversions are recently being witnessed and ministry to over 2,000 pastors, clergy, and their spouses has been welcomed by a diverse cross-section of denominational leaders." ...

And with all of this there has come a renewing of commitment, and enlarging and clarification of spiritual vision, and a rekindled passion for Jesus and for the work of His kingdom. Some of the physical manifestations accompanying the renewal are unsettling for many people, leaving them feeling that they have no grid for evaluation and no map to guide them, which is a sort of safe way of saying there are very bizarre things going on....

And so ... I went forward on the first night, because they said on the first night, "Anyone who's not been here before we'd like you to come first for us to pray for you." And I went up unapologetically and the lovely pastor said to me, "What would you like? What are you here for?" And I said, "I want everything that you've got. I've only got two days, and I've come from London," sort of defiantly. And behind this I was saying, "I've payed the fare and I'm determined to get my money's worth. So what will you do?" ...

The whole climate of this thing is surrounded with generosity. God has poured His Spirit out on a people in an improbable little church, and they are now spending their time from morning to night giving away as fast as they can what God is giving to them. And as new people hit town, and as pastors hover across the horizon, they sort of savour it as if it were fresh meat and they just long to come to you and lay their hands on you and give you all that God has given them, which I take to be a mark of the Lord. I just take it to be the generosity of Jesus to His people....

These are ordinary people ministering in the name of an extraordinary God. And their pastor, John Arnott has said, "God is just using nameless and faceless people to minister His power in these days." And that's what I love. There is no personality attached. There's no big name involved. There's no one church that's got a corner in the market. This is something that Jesus is doing. And the people and the church are simply preoccupied with the person and the power of the Lord Jesus. No personalities. Just Him. And I love that, because I'm tired of all that stuff. I'm tired of the heroes and the personalities. I just want Jesus. I just want Him and His Church straight. And that's what I think I received. I saw the power of God poured out, just as it was in the book of Acts, and as I said this morning, I didn't see tongues of flame, but I suspect it was because I wasn't looking. And I have heard recently in this country of a meeting which took place where the Spirit of God was poured out and the building shook. The building shook, and three separate witnesses quite independently, came home and said the building actually shook. So we're in the days of the New Testament. This is kingdom stuff, and it's glorious. But it's not new.

And so I scurried back to Scripture and I scurried back to Church history and I have discovered glorious things in the writings of Jonathan Edwards, who was the initiator of the Great Awakening in America during the mid-eighteenth century, and he wrote this, which is remarkably similar to what I saw in Toronto just last week, two weeks ago. "The apostolic times seem to have returned upon us. Such a display has there been of the power and the grace of the Spirit." Jonathan Edwards speaks of extraordinary affections—of fear, sorrow, desire, love, joy, of tears, of trembling, of groans, loud cries, and agonies of the body, and the failing of bodily strength. He also says we are all ready to own that no man can see God and live. If we, then, see even a small part of the love and the glory of Christ, a very foretaste of heaven, is it any wonder that our bodily strength is diminished? ...

I have discovered a new heroine in the last few days, who is the wife, or was the wife, of Jonathan Edwards. And she was a very godly and wonderful woman. And she fell under the power of the Spirit of God to such a degree in the 1740s, that for seventeen days, she was insensible. She was drunk for seventeen days. She could do nothing. (Now the Baptist pastor in Toronto had had to do all the school runs and all the school picnics for two days, because his wife was out for the count for forty-eight hours. And he was driving, and he was packing the lunches, and he was doing their homework—he was doing everything and he said, "God, when are you going to lift off my wife, so that this home can get back into order?") But poor Jonathan Edwards had seventeen days in which his wife was insensible. And on one occasion she decided it was time to arise from the bed and to try and minister to the household, and they had a guest. So she got dressed in her best...and she went downstairs and lurching a little while, and as she passed the study where the door was open and Jonathan Edwards was talking to his friend about the Lord, as she heard the name of Jesus, her bodily strength left her, and she hit the floor. So they carried her back to bed, and there she stayed. And as it's said in the history books, no one recorded who made the lunch. So this thing is taking people over in the most remarkable way. And at the end of this time, Jonathan Edwards' wife said, "I was aware of a delightful sense of the immediate presence of the Lord, and I became conscious of His nearness to me, and of my dearness to Him." And I think it's this one phrase that has impressed itself upon my Spirit in the last week, and what I think is the key to this whole thing, is that the Lord in His mercy is pouring out His Spirit in order to persuade us, His people, of "His nearness to me, and of my dearness to Him." ...

I heard a story just this afternoon of a woman who had left a meeting rather as I had done, but she was reeling, and unwisely, she decided to drive home. This was all over the place, and she was stopped by the police. Honest to God, this is true. She was stopped by the police, and she got out of the car, and the policeman said, "Madam, I have reason to believe that you're completely drunk." And she said, "Yes, you're right." So he said, "Well, I need to breathalyse you," so he got his little bag, and as she started to blow into it, she just fell to the ground laughing. At which point, the policeman fell, too, and the power of God fell on him, and he and she were rolling on the freeway laughing under the power of God. And he said,

"Lady, I don't know what you've got, but I need it," and he came to church the next week and he found Jesus. He got saved.

And this is happening. People are going out and telling each other about Jesus with a recklessness that they've never known before. I don't know about you, but when people say "evangelism" the hairs in the back of my neck go up and I get guilt and I feel awful and I feel destroyed and defeated. Evangelism is a breeze, people. It's such fun like this. So there was a woman who had left one of the meetings and she had been laughing on the floor for two hours, and she got really hungry. So she went to the Taco Bell...and she sat down...and she looked across, and she saw a whole family eating burritos. And she said to them, ... "Do you want to be saved?" And they all said, "Yes!" All of them! And they were all saved and led to Christ on the spot.

And another man left a meeting and he went into a restaurant, and a man was watching him, and for about ten minutes, he watched him. And he had this...young man who came up to him and said, "Excuse me, but are you a Christian?" And this chap had just left the meeting—he said, "You bet." And he said, "Well, my wife has just left me. I've just lost my home. I've just lost my job, and I'm about to take my life. ... What can help me?" And he led him to Christ. And...this is good news, people. This is news for the people out there. People are getting saved right and left. And they are now discovering even in the Toronto area that there are several hundreds of people that are getting saved. People right and left are coming to know Jesus, because Jesus is the joy of our lives. It's a wonderful, wonderful thing....

People are being restored by the mercy and the sweetness of God. And, quite honestly, whether one stands or falls, whether one laughs or cries, whether one shakes or stands still, whether you go down could matter not, it just doesn't matter a bit. It doesn't matter how you go down. What matters is how you come up. It doesn't matter what goes on in the outside.

What counts is what Jesus is doing in our bodies and in our souls, in our hearts and in our spirits.

We have a woman in my prayer group who is a hair dresser. And she's married to a Muslim, and her life is not easy. And she said that in the course of the last week, she's been reading her Bible like never before. But she said, "I'm not reading it." She said, "I hear the voice of Jesus reading it to me. As if I were a child, Jesus reads me His book." Wonderful things....

I think if we come receptive and childlike, there is infinite blessing for the people of God at this time. I've discovered in myself a love for Jesus more than ever. I've discovered in myself an excitement about the kingdom I wouldn't have believed possible. I've discovered that I'm living in glorious days. There's no other time; there's no other place where I would have chosen to be born and to live than here and now (Riss 1995).

The church newsletter describing that Sunday's services circulated widely and triggered publicity in the media. Crowds flocked to the church in the following weeks, especially ministers. An HTB staff member referred to the "Toronto Blessing," a term the media quickly adopted to describe this enthusiasm and fervor for God. This renewal, refreshing, or touch of revival spread to over 7,000 churches in England within two years.

Along with other expressions of the deep impact of God's Spirit, this blessing helps to bring fresh vitality to Christian life and witnessing around the world.

## 1994

### *August 14—Sunderland, England (Ken Gott)*

Ken and Lois Gott, founders of Sunderland Christian Centre (SCC) in 1987 in the northeast of England, felt dry and worn out in 1994. Ken Gott and four other Pentecostals visited Holy Trinity Brompton in London. The Presence of God among

Anglicans humbled and amazed those Pentecostals. Andy and Jane Fitz-Gibbons wrote in *Renewal* (Apr. 1995, p. 11), that:

> Stereotypes were shattered as Ken and the other Pentecostals received a new baptism in the Spirit at the hands of Bishop David Pytches. The change was so profound in Ken that the members at SCC took up an offering and sent Ken, Lois and their youth leader for a week to Toronto. Like most of us who have made the same pilgrimage, they were profoundly touched, soaking in God for a week, never to be the same again.

The Fitz-Gibbons described the result:

> On August 14th, the first Sunday morning back from Toronto, the effect on the church was staggering. Virtually the whole congregation responded to Ken's appeal to receive the same touch from God that he and Lois had received. They decided to met again in the evening, although normal meetings had been postponed for the summer recess. The same experience occurred. They gathered again the next evening and the next...in fact for two weeks without a night off. Quickly, numbers grew from around a hundred-and-fifty to six hundred. Word reached the region and, without advertising, people began the pilgrimage to Sunderland from a radius of around 70 miles.

> By September a pattern of nightly meetings (bar Mondays) was established and each night the same overwhelming sense of God was present. That pattern has continued ever since, with monthly leaders' meeting on a Wednesday or Thursday afternoon (with usually around 300 in attendance) and a daily "place" of prayer being added.

> The effect on many churches and on thousands of individuals has been profound (Fitz-Gibbons 1995, 15).

The church began two meetings a day with a daily afternoon prayer meeting in January 1995. Many former criminals have been saved, and crime has dropped in the community.

Philip Le Dune, an associate pastor at Sunderland, sent this e-mail message (edited here) in August 1996:

Sunderland Christian Centre is located in a high density low cost housing area with all the problems associated with inner city deprivation. Prior to the start of Renewal we had had very little contact with the local population, and gave very little indication that we really wanted anything to do with them! The church was heavily protected against burglary with shutters and polycarbonate windows, and a high security fence and video cameras helped the security guards protect the cars— not a very welcoming sight to any would-be church attenders from the area. Our neighbours saw us turning up in our nice cars, wearing our smart clothes and carrying big black bibles. Many of the on lookers had no car, no nice clothes and some had no food.

Renewal has changed us forever. When God pinned a local gangster to the floor of the church one evening, only God knew that he was soon to be employed by the church, together with his wife, as youth workers. They now hold daily "meetings" with the people from the local community who are increasingly coming to see SCC as "theirs".

Recently the atmosphere in the youth club, held upstairs in the church hall while the Renewal meetings are held in the sanctuary downstairs, changed significantly. The youths, many of whom are already well experienced in criminal activities, had begun to take less interest in the usual youth club activities like pool and became much more interested in the ministry time. …Last week all of the kids decided to stay behind for prayer and the Holy Spirit turned up! One young lad, aged about 12, named Billy received prayer, and the Holy Spirit laid him out on the carpet.

Billy is notorious in the area and is considered by many, including his social workers to be beyond control. He has tried to break in to the church on numerous occasions and has been involved in petty theft as well as assaulting members of the church staff! Despite this he has been welcome to join with his peers in the youth meeting and has been enjoying himself! A leader asked him, "Why do you come out for prayer Billy?" and he replied, "It's the only time in the week I feel clean." ...

Keep praying, as this is surely the start of the Youth Church that we want to establish here in Sunderland.

The awakening or refreshing or renewal that impacted Sunderland Christian Centre also spread to churches across Europe. As visitors from around the globe visited them and as they took teams to many countries, that same fire ignited people and churches worldwide. Then 1995 saw a further explosion of revival fire.

## 1995

### *January 1—Melbourne, Florida (Randy Clark)*

Five local churches in Melbourne, Florida, invited Randy Clark as guest speaker at the Tabernacle Church on New Year's day of 1995. Unusual revival broke out with large numbers of people falling down, laughing, weeping, and many dramatic physical healings. Thousands flocked to the meetings, which were being held six days a week. Pastors and musicians from 15 different congregations hosted the meetings in a new expression of cooperation and unity.

Randy Clark reported:

> In 1994 I spent about 150 [days] in renewal meetings. During that time I never was in a meeting which I felt had the potential to become another Toronto type experience. That was until I went to Melbourne, Florida [on] January 1, 1995. Another revival has broken out. Many sovereign things have occurred which indicate this place too will be [the site of] unusual renewal meetings. I shall share some of these.

> First, what made me expect something special at these meetings? I never schedule over four days for meetings, but I scheduled fifteen days for this meeting. Why? I believed there were things going on which indicated a major move of the

Spirit was imminent. The Black and White ministerial associations merged a few months prior to my going. The charismatic pastors had been meeting together for prayer for six years, and pastors from evangelical and charismatic and pentecostal churches had been meeting and praying together for over two years. There was a unity built which would be able to withstand the pressures of diverse traditions working together in one renewal/revival meeting.

The meetings are held at the Tabernacle, the largest church in the area. It holds 950 comfortably. This was Jamie Buckingham's church, now pastored by Michael Thompson. The church sanctuary is filled by 6:15 with meetings beginning at 7:00. About 1,200 are crowded into the sanctuary, another 150 fills a small overflow room, and another 200-300 sit outside watching on a large screen (Riss 1995).

The Christian radio station WSCF, FM 92 at Vero Beach, Florida, an hour's drive south of Melbourne, interviewed Randy Clark on Friday, January 6. About this interview, Randy Clark wrote:

During [the] interview a DJ fell out [under the power of the Spirit] in front of the station manager who was interviewing me. He shook violently. Other station employees fell out under the power. After we left the station kept on sharing [on the air] what was occurring live for hours. People were healed listening to the broadcast. Others came under conviction, drove to the station and gave their lives to God. Others were rededicated while listening. One man had to go home from work unable to continue driving his truck because the Spirit was so strong upon him (Riss, 1995).

The General Manager of the radio station, Jon Hamilton, wrote this circular letter:

January, 1995. Dear Friend of Christian FM 92:

I had already put the finishing touches on my first letter of 1995. I really liked it. It was full of optimism and inspirational resolutions for the New Year.

It will never make it to the printer.

Instead, I am compelled to offer to you a testimony and witness as to a most remarkable day. I pray that it may serve to encourage those who seek God, and terrify those who oppose Him.

January 6, 1995 began in a rather ordinary way. It was Friday, it had been a busy week, but I was looking forward to a slow day. As I was leaving the house, I actually told my wife, "There's not much on my calendar, I may try to take the afternoon hours off and come home early."

I had agreed to interview a pastor from St. Louis, Randy Clark, that morning. Randy was the guest speaker at The Tabernacle Church's renewal services nightly, and since "The Tab" is a good friend of FM 92 (and many other area churches were participating in the meetings), we had decided to clear a slot on the morning show for a brief interview.

My guest was one of the leaders of the so-called "Toronto Revival". I had read about the Toronto meetings, but frankly, I've heard a lot of "revival rumours" over the years and have learned not to pay much attention. Normally, I don't do the interviews myself, but I was feeling cautious and let the "morning guys" know I'd be there during the show.

The interview was innocent enough at first. The subject turned to a discussion of the Holy Spirit's manifest presence in a meeting (as opposed to His presence that dwells within our hearts always). Rather suddenly, something began to happen in the control room.

It began with Gregg. He was seated behind me listening, and for no apparent reason, he began to weep. His weeping turned to shuddering sobs that he attempted to muffle in his hands. It was hard to ignore, and Randy paused mid-sentence to comment "You can't see him, but God is really dealing with the fellow behind you right now." I looked over my shoulder just in time to see Gregg losing control. He stood up, only to crash to the floor directly in front of the console, where he lay shaking for several minutes.

I don't know if you have ever tried to conduct a radio interview in such circumstances, but let me assure you I never have. I was mortified. We have always attempted to avoid any extremes at FM 92, so it was difficult to explain to our listeners what was happening. I had always known Gregg to act like a professional, so I knew something was seriously going on. I did my best to recover the interview under the embarrassing circumstances. I thanked the guest and wrapped it up. (And thought of ways to kill Gregg later!)

After when we have a guest minister in the station, we ask him to pray for the staff. Before Randy Clark left, we asked him to say a word of prayer.

We formed a circle and began to pray for the staff one by one. My eyes were shut, but I heard a thud and opened them to see Bart Mazzarella prostrate on the floor. He had fallen forward on his face. What amazed me most was that Bart was known to be openly sceptical. He simply did not accept such things. Within seconds, another and another staff person went down. Even those that remained standing were clearly shaken.

When they prayed for me, I did not "fall down". What did happen was an electric sensation shot down my right arm, and my right hand began to tremble uncontrollably. My heart pounded as I became aware of a powerful sense of what can only be called God's manifest presence.

Remember, our staff is not primarily Charismatic. We are Episcopalian, Nazarene, Evangelical, Pentecostal...and a couple of "not quite sure". While I personally am associated with an Assembly of God church, I'm quite the skeptic when it comes to "weird stuff". I don't watch many evangelists on TV, because too often I am turned off by what I see. This was completely new to us.

Randy was scheduled elsewhere, so after just a few minutes of prayer, he thanked me graciously and left quickly. Our staff remained in the control room, staring at each other wide eyed, and hovering over Bart, who still appeared unconscious on the floor. (He was completely immobile for over half an hour.)

There was a sweet atmosphere of worship in the room, so I told someone to put one of the Integrity Worship CD's on air while we continued to pray together.

I thought the atmosphere would abate after a few minutes and return to normal…but instead, our prayers grew more and more intense. The room became charged in a way that I simply cannot describe. After an hour of this, we realized that it was 10:30, the time we normally share our listener's needs in prayer.

I switched on the mike, and found myself praying that God would touch every listener in a personal way. After prayer, with great hesitation I added "This morning God has really been touching our staff, so we've been spending the morning praying together. If you're in a situation right now where you are facing a desperate need, just drop by our studios this morning and we'll take a minute to pray with you." This was the first time we had ever made such an invitation.

This is where everything went haywire.

Within a few minutes, a few listeners began to arrive. The first person I prayed with was a tall man who shared with me some tremendous needs he was facing. I told him I would agree with him in prayer. As I prayed for his need, a voice in my head was saying "It's a shame that you don't operate in any real spiritual gift or power. Here's a man who really needs to hear from God and you've got nothing worth giving him!" I continued to pray, but I was struggling. I reached up with my right hand to touch his shoulder, when suddenly he shook, and slumped to the floor. (He lay there without moving for over 2 hours.) I was shocked and shaken.

Two others had arrived at this point, and staff members were praying with them. Suddenly they began weeping uncontrollably, and slumped to the floor. This scene was repeated a dozen times in the next few minutes. It didn't matter who did the praying, whenever we asked the Lord, he immediately responded with a visible power, and the same manifestations occurred.

I didn't know whether to be terrified or thrilled, but clearly, something completely unusual was going on. A young man cautiously entered the room, and began to tell us that he was "just happening" to be scanning the radio dial when he heard "something about prayer". He reported that he was immediately overcome with conviction. Years before, he had contemplated going into the ministry, and had even attended a couple of years at a Christian College, but he had since strayed from God. As a chill of conviction swept him, he felt God suddenly tell him it was now or never. He drove to the station. We prayed with him to receive Christ as Lord, and afterward, he too slumped to the floor.

One by one they came. We continued to play praise-oriented music, and every hour (sometimes on the half-hour) we'd invite people to come.

Fairly early in all this, we ran out of room. The radio station floor was wall to wall bodies...some weeping, some shaking, some completely still. People reported that it was like heavy lead apron had been placed over them. They were unable to get up. All they could do was worship God.

Fortunately, our offices are inside of the complex at Central Assembly, so when the crowd began to grow, we moved across into the Church, leaving the radio station literally wall to wall with seekers.

Some teachers at Indian Christian School had heard what was happening, and asked us to pray for certain children they were bringing in the room. As we prayed for the kids, many began to shake and fall to the floor. Some would begin to utter praises to God. Others lay completely immobile for periods of over an hour. (If you've ever tried to make a seven year old lay still, you know it's a miracle!) A few simply experienced nothing at all.

By now I was convinced that we were experiencing a bona fide move of God. I had read about such manifestation experiences being common in the revival meetings of great men like Jonathan Edwards and John Wesley. I had also read of the great camp meeting revivals in the early 1800's, where thousands upon thousands experienced being "slain", but I never imagined I would really live to see it.

The crowd continued to grow, and lines began to form. The power of God continued to fall on those coming. It was almost like being in a dream. I would look up and see our staff members...eyes red, faces puffy, and hands trembling, but with a fire in their eyes and the power of God upon them. I couldn't believe it was the same people I knew and worked with. In a matter of hours, something we never even dreamed of (much less aspired to) was happening.

The floor in front of the sanctuary was soon covered with men and women, boys and girls. The aisles began to fill and we were pushing aside chairs for more floor space. Usually, one of our staff would "catch" the person as they fell, but on quite a few occasions we were caught by surprise and people fell hard on the floor. Frankly, we had no idea what we were doing. (I'm not sure I want to learn!)

At some point I looked up and saw a local Baptist Pastor walk in the door. I must confess that my first thought was, "Oh Boy...I'm in trouble!" While I knew this brother to be a genuine man of God, nevertheless I was concerned about how a fundamental, no-nonsense Baptist might take all these goings-on. (Besides, I didn't have an explanation to offer!) I walked up to greet him. He just silently surveyed the room, and with a tone of voice just above a whisper said, "This...is...God. For years I've prayed for revival.... This is God."

Within minutes more local pastors began to arrive. Lutheran, Independent, Assembly of God.... The word of what was happening spread like wildfire. As the pastors arrived, they were cautious at first, but within just minutes, they would often begin to flow in the same ministry. The crowd was growing and pastors began to lay hands on the seekers, where once again the power of God would manifest and the seeker would often collapse to the ground.

It did not seem to matter who did the praying. This was a nameless, faceless, spontaneous move of God. There were no stars, no leaders, and frankly, there was no organization. (It's hard to plan for something you have no idea might happen!)

Eventually, word of what was occurring reached Fred Grewe, the Melbourne pastor who had brought Randy Clark to the station earlier that morning. He and Randy, along with several other Melbourne pastors, jumped into the car and headed down to Vero Beach. At this point, we started broadcasting live from the Church. As the group from Melbourne arrived, more and more people also began to show up asking for prayer. It seemed like there were always more than we could get to.

Amazingly, unchurched, unsaved people were showing up. I got a fresh glimpse of the power of radio as person after person told us "I'm not really a part of any church...." A few were sceptical at first, and later found themselves kneeling in profound belief.

Sometimes people would rise up, only to frantically announce to us that they had been healed of some physical problem. One woman's arthritic hands found relief. Neck pains, jaw problems, stomach disorders and more were all reported to us as healed.

We have received at least a dozen verified, credible, reliable comments from people who told us that when they switched on the radio, they were suddenly, unexpectedly overwhelmed by the presence of God (even when they didn't hear us say anything). Several told us that the manifest presence of God was so strong in their cars that they were unable to drive, and were forced to pull off the road.

The "falling" aspect of this visitation was the most visible manifestation, but it was not falling that was important. What was important was the fact that people were rising up with more love for God in their hearts than ever before. They were being changed, and their hearts set ablaze. I have lost count of the numbers of people who told me of the change God worked in their life.

It's hard to imagine the impact this has had on our staff. It seems like God has almost given me a new staff, composed entirely of men and women with tremendous zeal for God. What is occurring in our local churches is even more amazing. My phone is ringing with the calls of excited pastors. At least a dozen area churches from completely different ends of the theological spectrum are already experiencing this powerful move in their church. The leaders of many, many other local fellowships have been visiting these churches to "check it out", and they too are being touched to "take it back" with them. It's almost like a tidal wave has hit this area of Florida.

If you are sceptical, I understand and forgive you. (I might have thrown a letter like this one away just days ago.) I share this only to try and offer a faithful rendition of what has really happened.

I only ask that you remain open to whatever God wants to accomplish through you. Christian history is full of accounts of those times when God elected to "visit" His people. When He has, entire nations have sometimes been affected. I believe you'll agree, our nation is ripe for such a revival. For such a time as this, let us look to God with expectancy.

With warm regards, I am, Sincerely Yours, Jon Hamilton General Manager" (Riss, 1995).

The revival in Melbourne continues with an astounding mixture of white, black, Asiatic, Hispanic, and American Indian people being touched by God, filled with the Spirit and witnessing to others.

## 1995

### *January 15—Modesto, California*
### *(Glen and Debbie Berteau)*

In January 1994, Glenn and Debbie Berteau, pastors of Calvary Temple Worship Centre in Modesto, California, strongly sensed that the Lord was going to give them revival there. Early in 1994, they challenged their congregation with that vision. After the "vision Sunday," individuals committed themselves to fast on specific days as the congregation became involved in a 40-day fast and prayer.

In early January 1995, they had a three-day fast. The church building remained open for prayer, and people prayed over names on cards left on the altar. Those able to do so met together daily for prayer at noon. Many pastors in the area began meeting each week to pray for the city.

On Sunday, January 15, 1995, the church began holding performances of the play, *Heaven's Gates and Hell's Flames.* It was scheduled for three days originally but continued for seven weeks with 28 performances. Jann Mathies, pastoral secretary of Calvary Temple, reported in April:

> As of this writing, approximately 81,000 have attended the performance with 90% each night seeing it for the first time. At time of printing, 33,000 decision packets have been handed out, and of that, (confirmed) 20,000 returned with signed decision cards. Over 250 churches have been represented with hundreds of people added to the churches in our city and surrounding communities in less than one month. People come as early as 3:30 pm for a 7 pm performance. There are over 1,000 people waiting to get in at 5 pm, and by 5:30 pm the building is full. Thousands of people have been turned away; some from over 100 miles away.... Husbands and wives are reconciling through salvation; teenagers are bringing their unsaved parents; over 6,000 young people have been saved, including gang members who are laying down gang affiliation and turning in gang paraphernalia.... The revival is crossing every

age, religion and socio-economic status…. We have many
volunteers coming in every day, and through the evening
hours to contact 500 to 600 new believers by phone; special
classes have also been established so that new believers may
be established in the faith (Riss 1995).

The play became a focus for revival in the area. Some
churches closed their evening services so their people could
take their unsaved friends there. One result is that many
churches in the area began receiving new converts and finding
their people catching the fire of revival in their praying and
evangelizing. One church added a third Sunday morning service to accommodate the people. Another church asked their
members to give up their seats to visitors. Bible bookstores sold
more Bibles than usual. A local psychologist reported on deep
healings in the lives of many people who attended the drama.

That play continues to be used effectively around the world.
For example, churches in Australia have performed the play
with hundreds converted in a local church. Hardened unbelievers with no place for church in their lives have been saved and
now live for God.

## 1995

### *January 22—Brownwood, Texas (College Revivals)*

Richard Riss gathered accounts of revival sweeping colleges across America beginning with Howard Payne University
in Brownwood, Texas.

On January 22, 1995, at Coggin Avenue Baptist Church in
Brownwood, Texas, two students from Howard Payne University, a Christian institution, stood up and confessed their
sins. As a result of this incident, many others started to confess
their own sins before the congregation. On January 26, a similar event took place on the campus of Howard Payne. Word
quickly spread to other colleges, and Howard Payne students

were soon being invited to other college campuses, which experienced similar revivals. From these schools, more students were invited to still other schools, where there were further revivals....

One of the first two students from Howard Payne to confess his sins was Chris Robeson. As he testified about his own life and the spiritual condition of his classmates, "People just started streaming down the aisles" in order to pray, confess their sins, and restore seemingly doomed relationships, according to John Avant, pastor of Coggin Avenue Baptist Church. From this time forward, the church began holding three-and-a-half-hour services. Avant said, "This is not something we're trying to manufacture. It's the most wonderful thing we've ever experienced." ...

At Howard Payne, revival broke out during a January 26 "celebration" service, as students praised God in song and shared their testimonies. Students then started to schedule all-night prayer meetings in dormitories....

Then, on February 13-15, during five meetings at Howard Payne, Henry Blackaby, a Southern Baptist revival leader ministered at a series of five worship services, attended by guests from up to 200 miles away. On Tuesday, February 14, more than six hundred attended, and students leaders went up to the platform to confess publicly their secret sins. About two hundred stayed afterward to continue praying. One of the students, Andrea Cullins, said, "Once we saw the Spirit move, we didn't want to leave." ...

After Howard Payne, some of the first schools to be affected were Southwestern Baptist Theological Seminary in Fort Worth, Texas, Beeson School of Divinity in Birmingham, Alabama, Olivet Nazarene University in Kankakee, Ill., The Criswell College in Dallas, Moorehead State University in Moorehead, Ky., Murray State University in Murray, Ky., Wheaton College in Wheaton, Ill., Louisiana Tech University in Ruston, La., Gordon College in Wenham, Mass., and Trinity Evangelical Divinity School in Deerfield, Illinois. In each case, students went forward during long services to repent of pride, lust, bondage to materialism, bitterness, and racism (Riss 1995).

These revivals continued throughout 1995. Details are given in *Accounts of a Campus Revival: Wheaton College 1995*, edited by Timothy Beougher and Lyle Dorsett (Wheaton: Harold Shaw Publishers, 1995).

## 1995

### *June 18—Pensacola, Florida (Stephen Hill)*

Over 26,000 conversions were registered in the first year of the "Pensacola Revival." Over 100,000 conversions have been registered in the first two years.

On Father's Day, Sunday, June 18, 1995, evangelist Stephen Hill spoke at Brownsville Assembly of God near Pensacola, Florida. At the altar call a thousand people streamed forward as the Holy Spirit moved on them. Their pastor, John Kilpatrick, fell down under the power of God and was overwhelmingly impacted for four days.

That morning service, normally finishing at noon, lasted until 4 p.m. The evening service continued for another five and a half hours. So the church asked Stephen Hill to stay. He changed his appointments, continued with nightly meetings, and relocated to live there, where he continues to minister in revival.

John Kilpatrick, pastor of the Brownsville Assembly of God Church, reported on their revival in 1997:

> Corporate businessmen in expensive suits kneel and weep uncontrollably as they repent of secret sins. Drug addicts and prostitutes fall to the floor on their faces beside them, to lie prostrate before God as they confess Jesus as Lord for the first time in their lives. Reserved elderly women and weary young

mothers dance unashamedly before the Lord with joy. They have been forgiven. Young children see incredible visions of Jesus, their faces a picture of divine delight framed by slender arms raised heavenward.

I see these scenes replayed week after week, and service after service. Each time, I realize that in a very real way, they are the fruit of a seven-year journey in prayer, and of two and a half years of fervent corporate intercession by the church family I pastor at Brownsville Assembly of God in Pensacola, Florida.

The souls who come to Christ, repenting and confessing their sin, the marriages that are restored, the many people who are freed from bondage that has long held them captive—these are the marks of revival and the trophies of God's glory. No, I am not speaking of a revival that lasted one glorious weekend, one week, one month, or even one year! At this writing, the "Brownsville Revival" has continued unbroken, except for brief holiday breaks, since Father's Day, June 18, 1995! How? Only God knows. Why? First, because it is God's good pleasure, and second, perhaps because the soil of our hearts was prepared in prayer long before revival descended on us so suddenly.

On that very normal and ordinary Sunday morning in June of 1995, I was scheduled to minister to my congregation, but I felt weary. I was still trying to adjust to the recent loss of my mother, and my years-long desire for revival in the church seemed that morning to be so far off. So I asked my friend, Evangelist Steve Hill, to fill the pulpit in my place. Although he was scheduled to speak only in the evening service, Steve agreed to preach the Father's Day message. We didn't know it then, but God was at work in every detail of the meeting.

The worship was ordinary (our worship leader, Lindell Cooley, was still ministering on a missions trip to the Ukraine in Russia), and even Brother Hill's message didn't seem to ignite any sparks that morning—until the noon hour struck. Then he gave an altar call and suddenly God visited our congregation in a way we had never experienced before. A thousand people came forward for prayer after his message. That was almost half of our congregation! We didn't know it then, but our lives were about to change in a way we could never have imagined.

We knew better than to hinder such a mighty move of God, so services just continued day after day. We had to adjust with incredible speed. During the first month of the revival, hundreds of people walked the aisles to repent of their sins. By the sixth month, thousands had responded to nightly altar calls. By the time we reached the twelfth month, 30,000 had come to the altar to repent of their sins and make Jesus Lord of their lives.

At this writing, 21 months and over 470 revival services later, more than 100,000 people have committed their lives to God in these meetings—only a portion of the 1.6 million visitors who have come from every corner of the earth...

If the prophecy delivered by Dr. David Yonggi Cho [given in 1991] years before it came to pass is correct, this revival, which he correctly placed as beginning at Pensacola, Florida, will sweep up the East Coast and across the United States to the West Coast, and America will see an outpouring of God that exceeds any we have previously seen. I am convinced that you, and every believer who longs for more of God, has a part to play in this great awakening from God (Kilpatrick 1997, ix-xiv).

Pastors, leaders, and Christians who have visited this revival have been returning to their churches ignited with a new passion for the Lord and for the lost. The awesome Presence of God experienced at Pensacola continues to impact thousands from around the world.

## 1995

### *October 27—Mexico (David Hogan)*

David Hogan, founder of Freedom Ministries, a mission to remote hill tribes in Mexico, told about the outpouring of the Spirit there in a sermon. This is part of his account:

I visited an outlying village. It took four hours in a 4 wheel drive and then two hours on foot, uphill—very remote. There's no radio, no T.V., no outside influences. I'm sitting up there in this little hut on a piece of wood against the bamboo wall on the dirt floor. Chickens are walking around in there. And this pastor walks up to me. He's a little guy, and he's trembling. He says, "Brother David, I'm really afraid I've made a mistake."

I hadn't heard of any mistakes. I was wondering what had happened in the last few days. He's got four little churches in his area. He said, "Man, it's not my fault. I apologise. I've done everything right, like you taught me. I pray everyday. I read the Bible. I'm doing it right. What happened is not my fault."

I said, "What happened? Come on, tell me what happened." He was trembling. Tears were running out of his eyes. He said, "Brother David, I got up in our little church. I opened my Bible and I started preaching and the people started falling down. The people started crying. The people started laughing. And it scared me. I ran out of the church."

That's what I was looking for. That's what I was waiting for, when God came in our work, not because somebody came and preached it, not because I said it was okay or not okay, because I was neutral about it. I knew it was all right, but I wanted to see it in our work not because I ushered it in, but because the Holy Spirit ushered it in. And he did.

I got together with my pastors and we made a covenant to do a month's fast in September 1995. This was as well as the three days on and three days off fast that we had been doing that year anyway, so we were ready for whatever God wanted to do. God hit me on the third day of that month of fasting, but I continued the fast and on the seventh day he hit me again greater than I've ever been hit in my life up to that point. But we continued fasting for the whole month.

We were in an awesome time. I didn't know how deep we were in the river of God. I'd been fasting for a month, and I didn't know what was happening. So I decided to get my pastors together in each section. We had groups of about 30-75 pastors in each section. I went into the most conservative area of our mission first, because I wanted to see what would happen. At the first meeting, with about 75 of my pastors I got up, I opened my Bible, and I shared one or two verses. Suddenly I felt: that's enough. They're used to me preaching two hours sometimes, but it hadn't been ten minutes.

I said, "Stand up." And they stood up. I said, "Receive the River of Life." You should have seen it! It looked like someone was hitting them with bats in the stomach and the head. But nobody was touching them. People were lying over benches, forward, backward, all over the place. I was trying to help, but I couldn't help. People were just flying everywhere. And these were ministers.

So I went through all the sections like that. I got into one section, and they were glad to see me. They hadn't seen me in a few months. I stood up. I opened my Bible. I read one verse about the fire of God, and the people started shaking. I thought, "Oh God, this is way out."

So I said, "Stand up." They tried to stand up. Some of them couldn't stand up. I just said the word "Fire." And the whole place fell. It was getting more and more scary to me. But people were getting healed without anybody touching them. A man in that meeting had been deaf for 27 years. I didn't know the man. He fell over and hit his head on a bench, and fell underneath the bench. He got up from there after a few minutes and he took off running out of the room. His ears had unstopped and he was running from the noise!

After I had been through all the sections, introducing this softly, it finally came time to call all the pastors together from the whole work. A couple of hundred of our pastors came. I wish you had been there to see what we saw! It was amazing.

On the first day, Wednesday 25 October 1995, there were about 200 pastors there, and the whole church that was hosting us. That made about 450 people. The first day was awesome. God hit us powerfully. There were healings. I was happy. The people were encouraged.

The second day, Thursday, was even better. It was stronger. I thought we were peaking out on the second day. I got there at eight o'clock in the morning and left at ten o'clock at night, and there was ministry all day. We were fixing problems, and God was working through the ministry. It was wonderful. But I tell you, I was not ready for the third day.

I don't have words to describe what happened to us when the Holy Spirit fell on us on Friday, October 27, 1995. If you had been there, you wouldn't have words to describe it either. It's an awesome thing I've been able to witness. The river of God is here, and it's full. There's plenty for all.

We were coming in from different areas. The Indians were all there. I didn't know they had been in an all night prayer meeting. I didn't know that the Holy Spirit had fallen on them and they couldn't get up. I didn't know that they had been pinned down by the Holy Spirit all night long, all over the place, stuck to the ground. Some of them had fallen on ant beds, but not one ant bit them.

I was staying about 45 minutes away. I got in my 4 wheel drive and as I drove there I began listening on the two-way radio. Some of our missionaries were already there, and were talking on the two-way radio saying, "What's happening here. I can't walk."

As I listened to them on the radio I felt power come on me. And the closer I came, the more heat I felt settling on me. I could feel heat, and I had my air conditioner going! When I got to the little church, I opened the door of the truck and instantly became hot. Sweat poured off me. I was about 300 yards from the church. The closer I got, the more intense was the heat. I could hardly walk through it, it was so thick. I'm talking about the presence of God. That was 7.30 in the morning!

I walked around the corner of the building. People were all over the place. Some were knocked out. Some were on the ground. Some were moaning and wailing. It was very unusual. By the time I got to the front of the church where the elders were I could hardly walk. I was holding on to things to get there. I could hardly breathe. The heat of the presence of God was amazing.

The people had been singing for two hours before I got there. At 8.15 on the morning of October 27, 1995, I walked up there and lay my Bible down on that little wobbly Indian table. Hundreds were looking at me. Some were knocked out, lying on the ground. I could hardly talk.

I called the nine elders to the front and told them the Holy Ghost was there and we needed to make a covenant together, even to martyrdom. We made a covenant there that the entire country of Mexico would be saved. They asked me to join them in that pact. When we lifted our hands in agreement all nine fell at once. I was hurled backward and fell under the table. When I got up the people in front fell over. In less than a minute every pastor there was knocked out.

We were ringed with unbelievers, coming to see what was going on. The anointing presence of God came and knocked them all out, dozens of them. Every unbeliever outside, and everyone on the fence was knocked out and fell to the ground. There were dozens of them. From the church at the top of the hill we could see people in the village below running out screaming from their huts and falling out under the Holy Ghost. It was amazing.

We always have a section for the sick and afflicted. They bring them in from miles around, some on stretchers. There were 25-30 of them there. Every sick person at the meeting was healed: the blind, the cancerous, lupus, tumours, epilepsy, demon possession. Nobody touched them but Jesus. There was instant reconciliation between people who had been against each other. They were laying on top of each other, sobbing and repenting.

I was afraid when I saw all of that going on. I looked up to heaven and said, "God what are you — ?" and that was the end of it. He didn't want to hear any questions. Bang! I was about three or four metres from the table. When I woke up some hours later, I was under the table. When I finally woke up my legs wouldn't work. I scooted myself around looking at what was going on. It was pandemonium! When some people tried to get up, they would go flying. It was awesome.

"And he showed me a pure river of water of life, clear as crystal, proceeding from the throne of God and of the Lamb" (Rev. 22:1). I saw that river. I actually saw the river, its pure water of life from God's throne. If I could see it again I would know it, I saw it, I experienced it, I tasted it.

We had five open-eyed visions. One small pastor was hanging onto a pole to hold himself up. He was there, but he wasn't there. He said to me, "Brother David, look at him. Look at him, Brother David! Who is it? Look how big he is! Oh, he's got his white robe on. He's got a golden girdle." It was Jesus. He said, "Brother David, how did we get into this big palace?"

I looked around. I was still on the dirt floor. I still had a grass roof over me, but he was in a marble palace, pure white. I crawled over to look at him. He was seeing things we could not see. Another of the elders, a prophet from America, who had been working with me for thirteen years, crawled over and we were watching this pastor who was in a trance. It was amazing.

The three of us were inside something like a force field of energy. Anybody who tried to come into it was knocked out. It was scary. The pastor said, "He's got a list, Brother David." And the pastor started reading out aloud from the list. I was looking around, and as he was reading from the list people went flying through the air, getting healed and delivered. It was phenomenal, what God was doing. And he's done it in every service in our work that I've been in since then. It's been over a year. It's amazing. Wonderful.

Between 150 and 500 people per month are being saved because of it, just through what the North American missionaries are doing (Hogan 1997, 33-39).

David Hogan reported these events in a sermon at the Christian Outreach Centre in Brisbane just over a year after that powerful visitation of God in their work. The awesome Presence of God continues among them.

## 1996

### *October 20—Houston, Texas (Richard Heard)*

Richard Heard led the Christian Tabernacle in Houston in growth from 250 to 3,000 members. On Sunday, October 20, 1996, a move of God exploded in the church and dramatically affected it.

During the previous year the church had placed a strong emphasis on knowing Christ intimately. That August of 1996 Hector Giminez from Argentina ministered there with great power and many significant healings. Awareness of the presence and glory of the Lord increased during October, especially with the ministry of an evangelist friend of Richard, Tommy Tenny, who was also to speak the morning of October 20. Richard was preparing to welcome him and had just read about God's promise of revival from Second Chronicles 7:14, when God's power hit the place—even splitting the Plexiglas pulpit.

He spoke about it by telephone in November 1996 with Norman Pope of New Wine Ministries in Pagosa Springs, Colorado, who put the transcript of the discussion on the Awakening e-mail. The following is an edited selection of Richard Heard's comments.

I felt the presence of the Lord come on me so powerfully I grabbed the podium, the pulpit, to keep from falling, and that was a mistake. Instantly I was hurled a number of feet in a different direction, and the people said it was like someone just threw me across the platform. The pulpit fell over that I had been holding for support, and I was out for an hour and a half. ... I could not move. And I saw a manifestation of the glory of God. ... There were thick clouds, dark clouds, edged in golden white and the clouds would—there would be bursts of light that would come through that, that would just go through me absolutely like electricity. ... There was literally a pulsating feeling of—as though I was being fanned by the presence of the glory of God. ... There were angelic manifestations that surrounded the glory and I didn't know how long I was out. They said later that I was there for an hour and a half.

In the meanwhile, all across the building people, they tell me, were falling under the presence of God. That's not something that has happened much in our church, but people were stretched out everywhere. ... We have three services on Sunday and people would enter the hallways that lead to the foyer and then into the auditorium and they would enter the hallways and begin to weep. There was such a glory of God and they would come into the foyer and not stop—they would just go straight to the altar—people stretched out everywhere. ... There were all kinds of angelic visitations that people had experienced. And we've got professional people in our church—doctors, professors, their bodies were strewn everywhere.

When I felt the glory of God lift, I tried to get up and couldn't. It was as though every electrical mechanism in my body had short-circuited. I couldn't make my hands or my feet respond to what I was trying to tell them to do. It was as though I was paralyzed. ... And we had one service that day, and the service literally never ended—it went all the way through the day until 2:00 that morning. It had started at 8:30, and we decided to have church the next night, and I didn't want to be presumptuous, but we went on a nightly basis on that order, just announcing one night at a time, and as we got deeper into the week I could begin to see that God was doing something that was probably going to be more extended....

There have been numerous healings. The evangelist didn't speak at all that Sunday. In fact, the entire week he spoke maybe twenty minutes. There's been a really deep call of God to repentance. People come in and they just fall on their faces....

We had a great choir. We're a multi-ethnic congregation. A Brooklyn Tabernacle kind of sound, if you're familiar with that. Great worship and praise. Sunday morning there wasn't a choir member standing on the platform. They were all scattered like logs all over the platform. And we go in—[musicians] begin to play, to lead us into the presence of the Lord, and they play very softly. Because of our background, usually our worship is very strong, very dynamic, a lot of energy. Not any more. It's like you're afraid to even lift your voice.

Like they—even the notes on the piano they want to play very gently and then the Lord sweeps in. Five nights last week I wasn't even able to receive an offering. So—I mean, when He begins to move there's not one thing you can do. You just get out of the way and let Him work....

We've cancelled everything that we had planned. We have a lot of outside activities. We have 122 ministries within the church that have helped our church to grow, and these ministries were primarily either for getting people here or holding people once they've converted. ... I was telling our staff— they were asking, "Are we going to have Christmas musicals and childrens' pageants ever?" And we do a big passion play every year that brings in thousands and thousands of people. And I asked them, "Why do we do all of this?" and they said, "Well, we want people to come here so they can encounter God." I said, "Look at what's happening. We've got people storming in here that we've never seen, never heard of, never talked to. And God's doing it in a way that is so far superior to what we could do that whatever we've got going on. We're cancelling everything," and that's literally what we've done.

... And there hasn't been a single objection. That's what amazes me.

I think that this is probably going to end up—whatever this season is that the Holy Spirit is bringing us through in terms of our commitment to Him and the deep searching of our own hearts, it has the feeling at this point like it's going to—like it's building toward even a greater evangelistic outpouring....

There's a big difference in renewal and revival. I had the same skepticism of the laughter. I was raised in a classical Pentecostal background. I saw that from time to time, but the latest thing—I just—something inside of me just had a difficult time with it. And [in our church, after this visitation] there are people that are laughing like crazy now, and, I mean, all of this stuff I said that I had reservations about and didn't particularly care to see—I mean it's just as though God has said, "This is My Church. It's not yours." And I see the reality of it now. I think it's going to end up turning strongly evangelistic. It has that feeling and a lot of people are coming and being saved each night. There are many being saved, and there's not even really an altar call made that distinguishes between people that are already saved—that just need renewal and those that need conversion [because] it's just so intense right now.

A year later people were still being converted, often 30-40 a week. Richard Herd commented that everywhere in the church the carpet is stained with the tears of people touched by God and repenting.

These kind of reports are beginning to multiply across America and around the world as the power of God moves upon His repentant people who seek Him above all else. Revival visitations ignite millions of people in the world today. Amid growing darkness, the light shines. The cross is still the power of God for salvation to all who believe. The risen Lord empowers His people with His Spirit, which was His final promise: "But you shall receive power when the Holy Spirit has come upon you; and you shall be witnessess to Me...to the end of the earth" (Acts 1:8 NKJ).

# Chapter Seven

# **Conclusion**

Flashpoints of revival have occurred repeatedly starting at Pentecost up to the innumerable flames of revival around the world today. The flames of Pentecost have never ceased. The light shines brightly in the darkness still, and that darkness has never put it out (see Jn. 1:5). Often it has seemed as though darkness had triumphed and that evil abounded, when suddenly God showed His mighty hand again and again, especially in answer to the earnest, believing, repentant prayers of His people.

Revival fires continue to spread through the earth. From that initial outpouring at Pentecost until now they are controversial, disturbing, and often confusing. They often look better from a distance in time and space. They may look and sound very messy close up. Revivals in the history books or in Africa sound wonderful! Revivals in your own backyard can be a headache.

Noisy outbursts of strange activities, such as speaking in tongues, may cause huge crowds to come and see what is going on, even before any preaching begins (see Acts 2:6). Preachers may have to explain that they and their friends are not drunk as everyone thinks they are (see Acts 2:15). Hundreds or thousands of brand-new Christians may suddenly invade your church with all the problems and possibilities they bring (see

Acts 2:41). People in authority may object violently to these disturbing developments, especially if they involve healing in Jesus' name without any doctor present, and thousands more believing in Jesus without even a New Testament to guide them (see Acts 4:1-4). Those are the messy and wonderful problems typical of revival.

This book briefly surveyed a little of that story from the evangelical revivals in the eighteenth century to the current revivals of the last few decades. Revivals still burst into flame in spite of rampant unbelief and the spread of evil or persecution. Flashpoints of revival have occurred in many places including Africa, Latin America, China, Korea, and the Pacific where hundreds of millions have become Christian in a few decades.

It is an astounding story. A small community of Moravians prayed around the clock in "hourly intercessions" for a century and sent out missionaries while Whitefield, Wesley, Edwards, and others fanned the flames of the Great Awakening. Revival ignited further missionary zeal in the nineteenth century when Finney, Moody, and others led widespread revivals as hundreds of thousands cried out to God in prayer. The awesome Welsh revival early in the twentieth century ignited revival fires around the world and ushered in a century of repeated outbursts of revival with hundreds of millions turning from darkness to light.

Revival historian Edwin Orr described these awakenings following the Great Awakening of 1727-1745, as the Second Awakening of 1790-1830 (*The Eager Feet*, fired with missionary commitment), the Third Awakening of 1858-60 (*The Fervent Prayer*, spread through countless prayer groups) and the Worldwide Awakening in 1900 (*The Flaming Tongue*, spreading the word around the globe).

The twentieth century saw further movements of revival and renewal with the amazing growth of the church globally. The Pentecostal rediscovery of New Testament ministry in the power of the Holy Spirit ignited revival fires across the world.

Following the dark days of two world wars, evangelists and revivalists such as Billy Graham, Oral Roberts, T.L. and Daisy Osborn, and others gained global exposure from 1947-1948. Another outpouring of revival and renewal surged through the 1970's with revivals in Canada, the Jesus People movement in America, charismatic renewal in the churches, and a fresh outpouring of mission and evangelism in developing nations, which launched people such as Reinhard Bonnke, Yonggi Cho, and many more in leading hundreds of thousands to the Lord and establishing massive churches and ministries.

The 1990's continue to see an acceleration of revival including the spread of revival from countries such as Argentina and from local American communities such as Pensacola.

Accounts such as the ones in this book raise other awkward questions. How much is of God? How much is just human reaction to the Spirit of God? How much is mere excitement and enthusiasm? How much is hysteria? How much is crowd manipulation? How much is demonic?

The answers to such questions can fall into two equally dangerous and opposite extremes. On one hand we may think that it is all of God, alone, when, in fact, there are always many human reactions and even demonic attacks mixed in with powerful revivals. On the other hand we may dismiss it all as emotional hype, psychological reactions and/or sociological developments, when, in fact, God has brought people from death to life and from darkness to light in huge numbers, permanently affecting their eternal destiny.

When the religious and political leaders in Jerusalem faced similar dilemmas, especially the boldness of uneducated and ordinary people with a flaming zeal for the Jesus whom those leaders had killed, they were not happy (see Acts 4:13-21). In fact, they wanted to kill those revivalists as they had killed Jesus. However, one of their more insightful leaders reminded them that they may end up fighting against God—a rather unequal match (see Acts 5:33-39).

May God grant us the *faith* to believe in our great God who is able and willing to do far more than anything we could ever ask or imagine (see Eph. 3:20-21), the *hope* that shines in a dark world where we desperately need God's grace to abound in revival (see Rom. 5:20-21), and the *love* to serve and bless one another as Jesus demands of us and as He Himself loves us (see Jn. 13:34-35).

Flashpoints of revival ignited the early Church and turned their world upside down (see Acts 17:6). Fire has fallen again and again in revivals, and still does. We need to be people full of repentance, humility, faith, vision, wisdom, love, and the fire of the Holy Spirit as we live for God in our moment in history.

# References

Allen, W.E., ed. (1948) *Short Life of Charles G. Finney*. Lisburn: Revival.

Arnott, J. (1995) *Keep the Fire*. London: Marshall Pickering.

Backhouse, R., ed. (1996) *The Classics on Revival*. London: Hodder & Stoughton.

Balcombe, D. (1991) *Hong Kong and China Report*. Hong Kong: Revival Christian Church.

Balcombe, D. (1994) *Hong Kong and China Report*. Hong Kong: Revival Christian Church.

Burgess, S.M. & McGee, G.B., eds. (1988) *Dictionary of Pentecostal and Charismatic Movements*. Grand Rapids: Zondervan.

Burke, T. and D. (1977) *Anointed for Burial*. Seattle: Frontline.

Chant, B. (1984) *Heart of Fire*. Adelaide: Tabor.

Duewel, W. (1995) *Revival Fire*. Grand Rapids: Zondervan.

Edwards, J. (1835) *The Works of Jonathan Edwards*. Vol. 1. 1974 edition. Edinburgh: Banner of Truth Trust.

Evans, E. (1969) *The Welsh Revival of 1904*. Bridgend: Evangelical Press.

Fisher, H.A. (1950) *Reviving Revivals*. Springfield: Gospel Publishing House.

Fitz-Gibbons, A. & J. (1995) *Something Extraordinary Is Happening*. Crowborough: Monarch.

Frodsham, S.H. (1946) *With Signs Following*. Springfield: Gospel Publishing House.

Gondarra, D. (1991) "Pentecost in Arnhem Land" in G. Waugh, ed. *Church on Fire*. Melbourne: Uniting Education, pages 14-19.

Grant, P.E. (1986) "Visitation and Vivifying in Vanuatu." Unpublished paper.

Greenfield, J. (1927) *Power From on High*. Reprinted 1950. London: Christian Literature Crusade.

Griffin, S.C. (1992) *A Forgotten Revival*. Bromley: One Day Publications.

Griffiths, A. (1977) *Fire in the Islands*. Wheaton: Shaw.

Hogan, D. (1997) "The River of God." *Renewal Journal*, No. 9, pages 33-39.

Howard, P.E. (1949) *The Life and Diary of David Brainerd*. Jonathan Edwards, ed. Reprinted 1989. Grand Rapids: Baker.

Hughes, S. (1990) *Revival: Times of Refreshing*. London: CWR.

Hyatt, E. (1997) *200 Years of Charismatic Christianity*. Tulsa: Hyatt.

Idle, C., ed. (1986) *The Journal of John Wesley*. Tring: Lion.

Jay, E., ed. (1987) *The Journal of John Wesley*. Oxford: Oxford University Press.

Kilpatrick, J. (1997) *When the Heavens Are Brass*. Shippensburg: Revival Press.

Koch, K. (1973) *Revival Fires in Canada*. Grand Rapids: Kregel.

Koch, K. (n.d.) *The Revival in Indonesia*. Grand Rapids: Kregel.

McQuillan, R. (1997) "Harvest Now." *Renewal Journal*, No. 9, pages 46-48.

Miller, R.E. (1988) *Cry for Me Argentina*. Brentwood: Sharon.

Mills, B. (1990) *Preparing for Revival*. Eastbourne: Kingsway.

Moody, W.R. (1900) *The Life of D.L. Moody*. New York: Revell.

Orr, J.E. (1973) *The Flaming Tongue (1900-)*. Chicago: Moody.

Orr, J.E. (1974) *The Fervent Prayer (1858-)*. Chicago: Moody.

Orr, J.E. (1975a) *The Eager Feet (1790-1830)*. Chicago: Moody.

Orr, J.E. (1975b) *Evangelical Awakenings in Africa*. Minneapolis: Bethany.

Osborn, H.H. (1991) *Fire in the Hills*. Crowborough: Highland.

Osborn, T.L. (1986) *Healing the Sick*. Tulsa: Harrison House.

Overend, R. (1986) *The Truth Will Set You Free*. Laurieton: S.S.E.M.

Pratney, W. (1994) *Revival*. Lafayette: Huntington House.

Pytches, D. (1989) *Does God Speak Today?* London: Hodder & Stoughton.

Riss, R.M. (1988) *A Survey of 20th Century Revival Movements in North America*. Peadbody: Hendrickson.

Robinson, S. (1992) *Praying the Price*. Tonvridge: Sovereign World.

Steele, R. (1984) *Plundering Hell*. Johannesburg: Sceptre.

Tari, M. (1971) *Like a Mighty Wind*. Carol Springs: Creation House.

Tari, M. & N. (1974) *The Gentle Breeze of Jesus*. Carol Springs: Creation House.

Trinder, D. (1994) "Spirit Wave." *Renewal Journal*, No. 3, pages 65-74.

van Bruggen, J. (1989). Unpublished correspondence.

Wallis, A. (1956) *In the Day of Thy Power*. London: Christian Literature Crusade.

Wessel, H., ed. (1977) *The Autobiography of Charles Finney.* Minneapolis: Bethany.

Whittaker, C. (1984) *Great Revivals.* London: Marshalls.

Wimber, J. (1994) "A Season of New Beginnings." *Vineyard Reflections*, May/June.

Wirt, S. (1975) *Knee-Deep in Love.* London: Coverdale.

Worldwide Evangelization Crusade. (1954) "This Is That." London: Worldwide Evangelization Crusade.

## Magazines

*Christian History.* #23 (Vol. VIII, No. 3, 1989) "Spiritual Awakenings in North America." Carol Stream: Christianity Today.

*Open Doors*, Australian circular, September 1993.

*Renewal Journal.* Brisbane: Renewal.

> #1 (1993:1) Revival
> #2 (1993:2) Church Growth
> #3 (1994:1) Community
> #4 (1994:2) Healing
> #5 (1995:1) Signs and Wonders
> #6 (1995:2) Worship
> #7 (1996:1) Blessing
> #8 (1996:2) Awakening
> #9 (1997:1) Mission
> #10 (1997:2) Evangelism

## Internet

Ahn, C. (1995) *The Wine Press*, Vol. 1, No.1 "Pastor's Note." http://www.grmi.org/churches/HarvestRock/

Riss, R. (1995) "A History of the Worldwide Awakening of 1992-1995." www.grmi.org/renewal/Richard_Riss/history.html

Waugh, G., ed. (1993) *Renewal Journal.* www.pastornet.net.au/renewal

# *Destiny Image*
# New Releases

## WHEN GOD STRIKES THE MATCH
*by Dr. Harvey R. Brown, Jr.*

A noted preacher, college administrator, and father of an "all-American" family—what more could a man want? But when God struck the match that set Harvey Brown ablaze, it ignited a passion for holiness and renewal in his heart that led him into a head-on encounter with the consuming fire of God.

Paperback Book, 160p. ISBN 0-7684-1000-2 (6" X 9") Retail $8.99

## THE LOST ART OF INTERCESSION
*by Jim W. Goll.*

How can you experience God's anointing power as a result of your own prayer? Learn what the Moravians discovered during their 100-year prayer Watch. They sent up prayers; God sent down His power. Jim Goll, who ministers worldwide through a teaching and prophetic ministry, urges us to heed Jesus' warning to "watch." Through Scripture, the Moravian example, and his own prayer life, Jim Goll proves that "what goes up must come down."

Paperback Book, 182p. ISBN 1-56043-697-2 Retail $8.99

## WORSHIP: THE PATTERN OF THINGS IN HEAVEN
*by Joseph L. Garlington.*

Joseph Garlington, a favorite Promise Keepers' speaker and worship leader, delves into Scripture to reveal worship and praise from a Heaven's-eye view. Learn just how deep, full, and anointed God intends our worship to be.

Paperback Book, 182p. ISBN 1-56043-195-4 Retail $8.99

## Available at your local Christian bookstore.
### Internet: http://www.reapernet.com

Prices subject to change without notice.

# D Destiny Image
# Revival Titles

## FROM HOLY LAUGHTER TO HOLY FIRE
*by Dr. Michael L. Brown.*
America is on the edge of a national awakening—God is responding to the cries of His people! This stirring book passionately calls us to remove the roadblocks to revival. If you're looking for the "real thing" in God, this book is must reading!
Paperback Book, 294p. ISBN 1-56043-181-4 Retail $9.99

## IMAGES OF REVIVAL
*by Richard and Kathryn Riss.*
"Revival" means many things to many people. But what is real revival actually like? In this brief overview, the authors examine the many images of revivals that have occurred throughout the years. God's moves upon His people are exciting and sometimes unexpected. Learn how revival could come to your community!
Paperback Book, 182p. ISBN 1-56043-687-5 Retail $8.99

## IN SEARCH OF REVIVAL
*by Stuart Bell.*
Will revival always look the same? Who will recognize it when it comes? What part do we play in bringing revival to our city? How do we sustain revival? *In Search of Revival* details how you can position yourself for the moving of God's Spirit. You'll see characteristics marking churches on their own quest. Get ready to see revival in a whole new way!
Paperback Book, 176p. ISBN 0-7684-1001-0 Retail $8.99

### Available at your local Christian bookstore.
### Internet: http://www.reapernet.com
Prices subject to change without notice.

# **D** *Destiny Image*
# Revival Titles

## SHARE THE FIRE
*by Dr. Guy Chevreau.*
Do you panic when you hear the word *evangelism*? Do you feel awkward "forcing" your opinions on another? All that changes when God abundantly and freely fills you with His Spirit! In *Share the Fire* you'll learn how God has intended evangelism to be: a bold and free work of Christ in you and through you!
Paperback Book, 182p. ISBN 1-56043-688-3 Retail $8.99

## THE CHURCH OF THE 3RD MILLENNIUM
*by Marc A. Dupont.*
Uncontrollable laughter, violent shaking, falling "under the Spirit"—can these things really be from God? Using examples from the ministries of Elijah, John the Baptist, and Jesus Himself, Marc Dupont shows that God often moves in ways that challenge traditional religious views or habits; He "offends the mind in order to reveal the heart." God's end-time Church shouldn't be satisfied with the status quo. We need to reach for more of God's Spirit—and not be surprised when He gives it to us!
Paperback Book, 182p. ISBN 1-56043-194-6  Retail $8.99

## GO INSIDE THE TORONTO BLESSING— *NEW VIDEO*
*by Warren Marcus.*
Award-winning filmmaker Warren Marcus takes you behind the scenes where you can experience a true look at this revival with footage that has never been filmed before. You will feel like you have a front row seat at the worship services. You will witness the special prayer time when many of the miracles occur. You will see unusual "manifestations"—like those reported in prior revivals. And you will hear first-person account after account of how God has dramatically changed people's lives in this revival.
1 video (approx. 60 min.) ISBN 0-7684-0082-1 Retail $19.99

### Available at your local Christian bookstore.
### Internet: http://www.reapernet.com
Prices subject to change without notice.

# **D** *Destiny Image*
# Revival Books

## LET NO ONE DECEIVE YOU
*by Dr. Michael L. Brown.*

No one is knowingly deceived. Everyone assumes it's "the other guy" who is off track. So when people dispute the validity of current revivals, how do you know who is right? In this book Dr. Michael Brown takes a look at current revivals and at the arguments critics are using to question their validity. After examining Scripture, historical accounts of past revivals, and the fruits of the current movements, Dr. Brown comes to a logical conclusion: God's Spirit is moving. *Let No One Deceive You!*

Paperback Book, 320p. ISBN 1-56043-693-X (6" X 9") Retail $10.99

## THE GOD MOCKERS
### And Other Messages From the Brownsville Revival
*by Stephen Hill.*

Hear the truth of God as few men have dared to tell it! In his usual passionate and direct manner, Evangelist Stephen Hill directs people to an uncompromised Christian life of holiness. The messages in this book will burn through every hindrance that keeps you from going further in God!

Paperback Book, 182p. ISBN 1-56043-691-3 Retail $8.99

## IT'S TIME
*by Richard Crisco.*

"We say that 'Generation X' does not know what they are searching for in life. But we are wrong. They know what they desire. We, as the Church, are the ones without a revelation of what they need." It is time to stop entertaining our youth with pizza parties and start training an army for God. Find out in this dynamic book how the Brownsville youth have exploded with revival power...affecting the surrounding schools and communities!

Paperback Book, 144p. ISBN 1-56043-690-5 Retail $8.99

## A TOUCH OF GLORY
*by Lindell Cooley.*

This book was written for the countless "unknowns" who, like Lindell Cooley, are being plucked from obscurity for a divine work of destiny. Here Lindell, the worship leader of the Brownsville Revival, tells of his own journey from knowing God's hand was upon him to trusting Him. The key to personal revival is a life-changing encounter with the living God. There is no substitute for a touch of His glory.

Paperback Book, 182p. ISBN 1-56043-689-1 Retail $8.99

## Available at your local Christian bookstore.

## Internet: http://www.reapernet.com

Prices subject to change without notice.

# **D**
## *Destiny Image*
## Revival Books

## WHEN THE HEAVENS ARE BRASS
*by John Kilpatrick.*
Pastor John Kilpatrick wanted something more. He began to pray, but it seemed like the heavens were brass. The lessons he learned over the years helped birth a mighty revival in Brownsville Assembly of God that is sweeping through this nation and the world. The dynamic truths in this book could birth life-changing revival in your own life and ministry!
Paperback Book, 168p. ISBN 1-56043-190-3 (6" X 9") Retail $9.99

## WHITE CANE RELIGION
### And Other Messages From the Brownsville Revival
*by Stephen Hill.*
In less than two years, Evangelist Stephen Hill has won nearly 100,000 to Christ while preaching repentance, forgiveness, and the power of the blood in what has been called "The Brownsville Revival" in Pensacola, Florida. Experience the anointing of the best of this evangelist's life-changing revival messages in this dynamic book!
Paperback Book, 182p. ISBN 1-56043-186-5 Retail $8.99

## PORTAL IN PENSACOLA
*by Renee DeLoriea.*
What is happening in Pensacola, Florida? Why are people from all over the world streaming to one church in this city? The answer is simple: *Revival!* For more than a year, Renee DeLoriea has lived in the midst of the revival at Brownsville Assembly of God. *Portal in Pensacola* is her firsthand account of this powerful move of the Spirit that is illuminating and transforming the lives of thousands!
Paperback Book, 182p. ISBN 1-56043-189-X Retail $8.99

## Available at your local Christian bookstore.
### Internet: http://www.reapernet.com
Prices subject to change without notice.

# Exciting titles by Don Nori

## THE POWER OF BROKENNESS

Accepting Brokenness is a must for becoming a true vessel of the Lord, and is a stepping-stone to revival in our hearts, our homes, and our churches. Brokenness alone brings us to the wonderful revelation of how deep and great our Lord's mercy really is. Join this companion who leads us through the darkest of nights. Discover the *Power of Brokenness*.
Paperback Book, 168p. ISBN 1-56043-178-4 Retail $8.99

## THE ANGEL AND THE JUDGMENT

Few understand the power of our judgments—or the aftermath of the words we speak in thoughtless, emotional pain. In this powerful story about a preacher and an angel, you'll see how the heavens respond and how the earth is changed by the words we utter in secret.
Paperback Book, 192p. ISBN 1-56043-154-7 (6" X 9") Retail $10.99

## HIS MANIFEST PRESENCE

This is a passionate look at God's desire for a people with whom He can have intimate fellowship. Not simply a book on worship, it faces our triumphs as well as our sorrows in relation to God's plan for a dwelling place that is splendid in holiness and love.
Paperback Book, 182p. ISBN 0-914903-48-9 Retail $7.99
*Also available in Spanish.*
Paperback Book, 168p. ISBN 1-56043-079-6 Retail $7.99

## SECRETS OF THE MOST HOLY PLACE

Here is a prophetic parable you will read again and again. The winds of God are blowing, drawing you to His Life within the Veil of the Most Holy Place. There you begin to see as you experience a depth of relationship your heart has yearned for. This book is a living, dynamic experience with God!
Paperback Book, 182p. ISBN 1-56043-076-1 Retail $8.99

## HOW TO FIND GOD'S LOVE

Here is a heartwarming story about three people who tell their stories of tragedy, fear, and disease, and how God showed them His love in a real way.
Paperback Book, 108p. ISBN 0-914903-28-4 (4" X 7") Retail $3.99
*Also available in Spanish.*
Paperback Book, 144p. ISBN 1-56043-024-9 (4" X 7") Retail $3.99